The Confrontational Parent:

A Practical Guide for School Leaders

Dr. Charles M. Jaksec III

EYE ON EDUCATION
6 DEPOT WAY WEST, SUITE 106
LARCHMONT, NY 10538
(914) 833–0551
(914) 833–0761 fax
www.eyeoneducation.com

Library of Congress Cataloging-in-Publication Data

Library of Congress Cataloging-in-Publication Data

Jaksec, Charles.
    The confrontational parent : a practical guide for school lead-
    ers / Charles M. Jaksec, III.
        p. cm.
    Includes bibliographical references (p.)
    ISBN 1-930556-51-9
    1. School administrators--Handbooks, manuals, etc. 2. Com-
    munication in education--Handbooks, manuals, etc. 3. Par-
    ent-teacher relationships--Handbooks, manuals, etc. 4.
    Agressiveness--Handbooks, manuals, etc. I. Title.

LB2831.8 .J35 2003
371.19'2--dc21

10 9 8 7 6 5 4   2002040764

Editorial and production services provided by
Richard H. Adin Freelance Editorial Services
52 Oakwood Blvd., Poughkeepsie, NY 12603-4112
(845-471-3566)

Acknowledgments

My wife, Samantha, is a wonderful spouse and amazing mother. She is my advisor and also the most dedicated educator I have ever met. In my life, the presence of Sam and my two beautiful children, Jordan and Chuckie, make me the luckiest person in the world.

My mother, Dolly, has taught me lessons that I always draw upon. There is no better mother. My brothers, Greg, Chris, and Stephen, are consummate professionals who never fail to lend advice and support.

I would like to acknowledge Joe Brown, Jeff Smith, Beth Larcom, Vito Ricciardi, Randy Poindexter, Jackie Heard, Theo Schmid, and Diane Simpson (who doubles as my mother-in-law) for their friendship and advice. I also want to thank my supervisor Ken Gaughan and coordinators Dawn Gullatt and Mike Levine, who have always been steady sources of support during my professional endeavors.

Dr. Charlie Council and Dr. John Hilderbrand from the Florida Education Research Council (FERC), and the Florida Association for School Administrators (FASA) provided avenues for my studies. Thank you for the opportunity to conduct my research.

Dr. Bob Dedrick has been involved with this project since its inception. Anyone who engages in a research-related project would be blessed to have a mentor and friend who would take the time to share his expertise with this amount of enthusiasm and patience. I will always be grateful for his efforts.

Herman Valdes gave me the inspiration to engage in this project. He is widely known as a coaching "legend" in the state of Florida. I think that this athletic description shortchanges him though, since educationally, Herman has also inspired countless people. He is never afraid to express his feelings about what is right and why it is right. He is a "hugger" in an era of "handshakers." Sadly, Herman prepares to retire in the next few years; he can't be replaced.

Michael Braun provided the artwork used in the background on the front cover. He can be reached at mbraun1@tampabay.rr.com.

Bob Sickles and Eye on Education Publishers gave me the opportunity to make my project known. I will always appreciate their interest and support.

Finally, thank you Jesus, Mary, Joseph, and Jude for your love.

Dedication

To my father—the gentlest parent.

Table of Contents

About the Author

Chuck Jaksec is a school social worker with the Hillsborough County School District in Tampa, Florida. He is also a member of the school district's crisis intervention team. He has authored journal and magazine articles on the topic of parental aggression toward administrators. He has also authored articles on school crisis intervention. Jaksec has engaged in presentations on these topics nationally.

Jaksec received his undergraduate degree in Social Work from Slippery Rock University of Pennsylvania, where he also received a Masters Degree in Counseling Services. At the University of South Florida, he received an Ed.S. in Counselor Education and a Ph.D. in Curriculum and Instruction. Jaksec resides in Tampa, Florida with his wife Samantha and their two children, Jordan and Michael.

Introduction

On what I considered just another school day a few years ago, I wandered into a principal's office for a routine after-school chat regarding the day's happenings. To my surprise, I encountered an emotionally shaken and thoroughly frazzled individual, the principal himself! I was actually not accustomed to seeing this person in a complete state of what I would consider a cross between fright and bewilderment. After several minutes, he regained his composure and explained that during dismissal a parent in the school parking lot verbally accosted him. The irate parent used profanity and made physical threats toward the principal apparently because the parent had been told to move his car. The parent, a physically imposing individual, then exited the campus.

The principal then proceeded to ask me, "Does anything exist on the topic of parents attacking school administrators?" After I jokingly informed him that I wasn't a walking literature review, I said that I might look into this topic at some time in the future—the distant future. What struck me about this incident, however, was that this highly confident, and usually unflappable principal (also a highly recognized 30-year coaching veteran) indicated that, for the first time in his career, he feared for his safety. He stated, "I really don't know if this is worth it anymore." As an educator, this brief statement made me uncomfortable. I concluded that if thoroughly competent principals decide "it's not really worth it" and leave the field of education, then the real victims are the students. As a school social worker and crisis intervention team member, I am aware of the impact of school administrators and their "trickle down" effect upon the overall school population.

Several months elapsed, and I decided to formally explore the topic of parental aggression toward school administrators. I discovered that research indeed existed, but much of it lacked depth and was not comprehensive or empirically based. I began to consider this as an opportunity to engage in research that examined a topic that was now becoming quite intriguing. I decided that my next step would be to write grants that were eventually funded by the Florida Educational Research Council. During the next three years, I conducted research studies that examined parental aggression toward school administrators in the 12th largest school district in the United States and another statewide study involving all 67 school districts in the state of Florida.

As I continue to write and present at the local, state, and national level on the topic of parental aggression toward school administrators, I have come to realize that this obscure issue is actually one of immense interest to school administrators. On countless occasions, individuals—not limited to school administrators—have informed me that this issue urgently requires more attention by school districts. With that in mind, I decided to write a book that would assist school administrators in their interactions with aggressive parents. The book, I vowed, would be research-based but practical in its application. It would also include suggestions and techniques that could prove useful to administrators as they conduct their duties in an increasingly volatile workplace. Finally, this book shares the wisdom and experiences of school administrators that I have had the fortune of working with, and presenting to, over the course of 18 years.

While writing this book, I made several assumptions. First, I assume that individuals reading this book have had previous experiences with confrontational or aggressive parents and, second, that individuals reading this book are competent, dedicated school administrators. To achieve the status of school administrator, one usually achieves a graduate degree and has some form of teaching experience. In sum, readers of this book are for the most part "people persons" with a wealth of skills and experiences on how to interact or not interact with people.

I dislike a "25-step" approach to anything, and my ability to memorize anything over five steps is slowly eluding me as I age. That being said, I promised myself that I would not author a cookbook type effort for dealing with confrontational or aggressive parents. I do, however, provide methods for interacting with these parents. I have chosen to identify and discuss realistic issues that affect the administrator's interaction with aggressive parents. I sincerely hope that this book, in some way, makes a turbulent situation a little less taxing for you.

1

The Confrontational Parent

Friday's school day is about to conclude and a well-deserved weekend slowly, but gratefully approaches. Unexpectedly, the school secretary calls your office and informs you that an irate parent is demanding to see you immediately. After making your way to the front office, it is all too apparent that your secretary's perception of the parent is accurate. You proceed to invite the parent to your office and discuss the matter, but as you attempt to present yourself as a concerned administrator, the parent could in fact, care less. Try as you may to remain composed, the parent makes a somewhat insulting statement regarding your capabilities as an administrator. The parent vows to go to the school board, but only after she secures the services of an attorney. Your composure is shaken and bingo, your weekend has been officially flushed down the toilet!

When I conduct presentations on parental aggression around the nation and provide this scenario, I am consistently amazed by the nods of confirmation I receive from school administrators. I am now convinced that this same irate parent has

1

visited 90 percent of the schools in the United States on Fridays between 2:00 p.m. and 4:00 p.m.

The problem with the aforementioned scenario is that your difficulties don't end as the parent leaves the campus. On the drive home you ask yourself, "Is she really hiring an attorney? What am I going to do if I'm fired? How long do I have until I can retire? Does this ever happen to my colleagues?" Incredibly and amusingly, these questions were not even considered five minutes before the confrontation with the parent. More frustrating, is the fact that you did nothing to warrant this kind of aggravation in the first place! Now however, these questions are at the forefront of your thoughts, and the knot in your stomach tells you that the majority of the weekend will be spent worrying about the parent's threats.

The Inevitable Battle

A major challenge for school administrators is to remain consummate professionals, who refuse to resort to intimidation or anger when dealing with parents who know how to "push buttons." An onerous task to say the least, since school administrators are normal people who naturally want to react in the exact manner directed at them.

While parental confrontations are inevitable, the school administrator's responsibility remains to carry on unscathed after these confrontations. It is reasoned that administrators are held to a "higher standard" of conduct; however the task of consistently remaining above the fracas can be extremely frustrating. Unfortunately, while many school board policies indicate that administrators need not tolerate emotional and physical intimidation by another adult, incidences of aggression continue. Consequently, school administrators find themselves questioning their own ability or willingness to interact with volatile parents. School administrators often raise questions such as: Am I alone in my encounters with aggressive parents? Do my colleagues also encounter these types of parental aggression? How often does parental aggression occur? What types of aggression are being identified in other schools? These questions will be answered in the following chapters, but before we address these questions, the concept of conflict should be briefly discussed.

What Causes Conflict?

Millions of our nation's children are assimilated into schools from a wide variety of cultures and experiences. As a result, school administrators must be sensitive to the fact that any number of variables can shape the behavior and performance of each student. This remains evident in the familiar phrase "no two children are alike." Conversely, it can be reasoned that "no two parents are alike," since like their children, parents are the product of the same types of diversity, with numerous variables influencing their behaviors and actions. It should come as no surprise then, that parents may view administrative decisions much differently than school administrators. The result of these divergent views is the creation of conflict.

The word "conflict" conveys a negative connotation, but conflict does not necessarily result in hostility. The parental disagreement or opposition does not actually create anger and hostility, rather, the manner in which the disagreement is handled results in hostility (Robbins, 1974).

Faced with the task of addressing a scholastic issue that may involve their child (or themselves), parents must interact and relate to school administrators who are capable of remediating the situation. The parent, in a sense, is dependent on the cooperation of the school administrator. The realization of this dependency often results in parental anger or frustration, which creates conflict that can deplete the school administrator's time, emotions, and resources (Margolis, 1988).

Conflicts and its Benefits

Interestingly, conflict can result in numerous advantages for the parties involved and need not result in damaged parent/administrator relationships. Rather, conflict can result in several advantages including: the creation of synergetic solutions to unfavorable situations, improved interpersonal relationships, and investment in the real problem and its solution.

Additionally, increased feelings of satisfaction and competency may also emerge. It is important to note that evading conflict may conceivably result in the problem lying dormant, with negative feeling emerging at inopportune times. Unfortunately, the opportunity to generate solutions is disregarded when conflict is avoided (Margolis, 1988). Margolis explains that conflict and anger may act as barometers of sorts, functioning as clear warnings that something is viewed as unsatisfactory. As a result, conflict and anger provide opportunities to remediate unsatisfactory or volatile situations.

The school administrator remains at the forefront of parental conflicts within the school. With this unenviable position, we tend to conjure thoughts of ugly verbal engagements with irate, irrational, and over-demanding parents who are impossible to appease. This is not necessarily accurate. According to Margolis (1988),

> It might be said that the quintessential test of an administrator's virtuosity is how well he or she manages conflict. School administrators face their most bracing tests and greatest opportunities in times of conflict. The challenge is not to suppress conflict, but to minimize its destructiveness and transform associated anger into positive force. (p. 3)

Subsequently, the campus contains no other individual in a more advantageous position to affect change through conflict. The school administrator—in a positive sense—can manipulate the conflict to the degree where anger is decreased and efforts can focus on the problem that originated the conflict.

The Same Old Comment

When discussing the topic of parental aggression, the most frequent comment I hear from school administrators is, "I can accept poor behavior from kids since they are only kids, but to accept childlike, aggressive behavior from an adult is another story." I tend to agree with this statement. It's not unreasonable for school administrators to expect adults to act maturely, and be capable of engaging in discussion of any issue that may arise, regardless of the intensity of the issue. Fortunately, the majority of parents maintain healthy relationships with their children's schools. In addition, if most school administrators were asked if their parents were non-problematic or problematic, the great majority would respond that parents are wonderful and supportive. It is important to realize that parents, like school administrators, often have the right to become frustrated or angry, but only if this anger is expressed in a constructive manner. On most occasions, aggressive parents' main objection is the way their child has been mistreated or wronged. Whether it is a complaint about their child's teacher or classmates, their child is their main concern. Unfairly but realistically, parents view school administrators as symbols of injustice done to their child. These "injustices" are usually parental misperceptions that administrators attempt to correct. Yes, parents are often held to a higher standard than their children, but every administrator can relate to a situation where the child actually acted in a more mature way and more appropriately than their parents. Unfortunately, some parents do not conduct themselves civilly, and school administrators remain at the forefront of these turbulent situations. Although in the minority and not encountered regularly, confrontational or aggressive parents require special attention from school administrators in the form of patience, perseverance, and skill.

The Need for Parental Support

Most administrators strongly desire parent involvement. Encouragingly, due in part to the Goals 2000: Educate America Act, an increase in parental support and interest has been identified (Patrikakou and Weissberg, 1999). Many states are also mandating various types of parental involvement in their schools (Black, 1998).

Parents are invaluable in the sense that they have a significant influence on their child's school success and academic performance. Parental involvement increases student academic achievement, improves motivation and behavior, and has positive effects on absenteeism and drop-out rates, and homework performance (Hester, 1989).

While it is evident that parental–school involvement benefits students, many obstacles interfere with these school–family partnerships. One obstacle may include the parent's own misperceptions about school. For example, the parent may have experienced his or her own childhood school difficulties in the areas of academic or behavioral performance.

Surprisingly, parents may not be comfortable with the extent of their school involvement. Public Agenda, a New York-based opinion research company recently conducted a survey revealing that while eager to volunteer time as chaperones or assistance for after-school activities, they expressed little interest in the governing of schools (Bradley, 1999). Only 25 percent of parents indicated that they would be "very comfortable" assisting in the planning of school curriculum.

Black (1998) explained that parental involvement can result in interference, and suggests that schools need to construct "bridges and buffers" for parental involvement. Bridges allow the parent to assist their child to succeed in school, and buffers allow school personnel to perform their jobs and exert their professional expertise. Black (1998) also calls for a "mutual trust" between the schools and parents. This trust would allow both factions to work together not against one another.

One thing is certain, school administrators realize that schools cannot and were never intended to function independently. Along with the realization of increased parental involvement is the inevitability of parental conflict. School administrators attempt to overcome these inevitable misunderstandings through a variety of approaches and philosophies inherent in his or her training and interpersonal skills.

The Difficult Person

Muriel Solomon (1990) identifies several emotional types of "difficult people." Descriptions include: "hostile/angry, difficult/underhanded, rude/abrasive, pushy/presumptuous, and complaining/critical. Realistically, at one time or another, every administrator interacts with one of these behavioral types. According to Rucci (1991),

> Unfortunately, people in a service-connected, public position, can not always afford to "turn-off" the person with whom they are interacting at a particular time, especially if it is with a parent or community member. For educators, there must be a calm and appropriate way to deal with those listed above or the results could be devastating to a large number of people....especially children and teachers. (p. 8)

As we will see in the following chapter, parents are becoming more vocal about their involvement in the educational process. School administrators, as a result, can no longer consider parents as outsiders, nor can administrators afford to ignore parental threats. Many public schools are currently structured to minimize public involvement, and an official voice from parents is inauspiciously absent. Unfortunately, parents are frequently excluded from decision making and their participation is limited. Conversely, parents can be vocal and demanding in their dealings with school personnel. Administrators are increasingly questioned as to their decisions. Parents view themselves as purchasers of public education; with the right to demand services from the school (Fege, 2000).

According to Fege (2000),

> Although schools have resisted change, the family has restructured. The result: 21st century families attempting to partner with 20th century organizations. The institutions of families and schools are crashing into each other, which leads to conflict and instability in school systems. (p. 40)

As schools become more readily accessible to parents and invite community partnerships, the need for "people conscious" school administrators increases. While the presence of conflict is inevitable, administrators who possess the skills necessary to interact with confrontational or aggressive parents allow the opportunity to maintain the critical parent/school relationship. A healthy school/parent relationship ultimately benefits the student, parent, and school community itself.

Discussion

1. Throughout your career as a school administrator, has conflict "changed" you? Are you more aggressive in your interactions with others, including aggressive parents or have you indeed come to view conflict as a way to recognize that something is unsatisfactory?

2. Think of your most volatile encounter with a parent. How did the situation resolve itself? Was the situation resolved at all?

3. Do you know a colleague who seems to thrive in conflict situations. What does this colleague do to make themselves especially suited for these situations?

2

Notions Related To Confrontational And Aggressive Parents

What makes an aggressive or confrontational parent such a formidable entity? According to Rucci (1991), "difficult people usually affect more than just one person with whom they are dealing at a particular moment. They can destroy a productive atmosphere and positive school climate in just seconds" (p. 8). While considering this very accurate statement, it might still be inaccurately reasoned that rather than dealing with aggressive parents, school administrators routinely encounter a wide variety of other, more critical challenges during a school day. The administrator's plate is routinely filled with issues related to student academic and behavioral performances, staff conflicts, financial matters, athletic events, community relations, or numerous other situations that must be addressed.

In addition, instances of parental aggression are not a daily occurrence, but when they do occur, skilled school administrators usually diffuse them. Thus, the question remains, "Does the issue of parental aggression deserve attention from our nation's school administrators?" To most accurately respond to this question, several notions must first be dispelled.

Notion One: Dealing with Aggressive Parents Is Similar to Any Other School Problem

Each school day, a myriad of problematic situations arise that require an administrator's patience, skill, and courage. Courage, however, is not often thought of as a necessary trait as administrators attempt to address various problems during the course of a routine school day. Interacting with an aggressive adult is however, frightening, and encounters with these adults certainly does require courage. Any adult, especially an aggressive adult, poses a viable threat and special challenges for a school administrator.

Within educational settings, interactions with students and staff occur so frequently that a certain comfort level is usually maintained. This enables administrators to interact with students or school personnel without negative emotional repercussions. In contrast, encounters with hostile parents frequently challenge school administrators to remain both composed and effective, especially when a parent becomes angry, accusatory, and openly questions the administrator's competence. This challenge remains difficult in most cases, but why?

First, parents are usually more knowledgeable, savvy, and capable of posing opposition than their children. Simply, parents are usually more formidable entities than their children, especially when angered. If not satisfied with their specific interaction with an administrator, a parent possesses the ability to take the problem to the "next level," that is, attorneys or school boards. This threat (or exercised option) may understandably prove to be emotionally discomforting to any school administrator. As mentioned in a previous chapter, many administrators share the belief that "kids will be kids, but adults should know better." This simple perception makes dealing with angry, unreasonable, adults all that much more difficult.

In cases of student or staff misconduct, administrators impose punishment in a variety of forms. Guidelines are followed and enforced, and the threat of reprimand hopefully prevents future misbehavior. In contrast, aggressive parents engage school administrators often with no sense of fear or reprimand. An assistant principal once disgustedly asked me this intriguing question, "Most people wouldn't even think of abusing a doctor, priest, or attorney, so why would they think its OK to abuse a school administrator?" Great question! One reason could be that these aforementioned professionals can tactfully—or not so tactfully—tell you to leave and go elsewhere if you perturb or anger them, and it is within their rights to do so. In contrast, a school administrator cannot choose parents or elect to dismiss them when they no longer feel like working with them when they become agitated or angered. Likewise, parents rarely remove their child from school upon disagreement with an administrator.

Compounding this disadvantage is the absence of school civility policies that prevent misbehaviors or aggressive approaches that could negatively affect school administrators. Subsequently, parents often engage school administrators with no understanding of "do's and don'ts." All too often, there exists no "line in the sand" to prevent aggressive behaviors. Indeed, encounters with confrontational or aggressive parents pose their own special problems that differentiate these types of problems from any other that the school administrator may face.

Notion Two: Dealing with Aggressive Parents Is Part of the School Administrator's Job

Most school administrators willingly make themselves available to hostile parents. Actually, this understandable since it could be reasoned, "Who else is going to handle the situation?" Administrators usually become involved in these conflicts since they sincerely believe that they are obliged to address any school related issue regardless of the situation or other party's disposition or intent.

Jeanette, a retired elementary school principal from Florida, comments, "Often, administrators are targeted since they are the ones who have to conduct the many conferences and sign all the paperwork. The administrator becomes the 'bad guy' since he or she must follow state laws and mandates, for example, special educational placements. Also, parents do not seek conferences with their child's teacher but go directly to the administrator, thus circumventing the teacher. The administrator does not discover the problem until it is too late. The parent, without an appointment, arrives 'hot under the collar' and demands that something be done immediately. If the problem is not immediately resolved, anger is directed toward the administrator."

Ideally, the administrator's involvement should cease when these encounters become abusive in any way, however, our nation's school administrators continue to become entangled in disputes with overly aggressive parents. Part of the reason could be perceived pressure from their superiors, that is, superintendents and school boards, who believe that all issues—regardless of their nature—should indeed be addressed by the school-based administrator. The message is clearly sent "it is part of your job to deal with irate parents." This is not to say that administrators should steadfastly refuse to engage angry individuals, however, the administrators should be given the opportunity to avoid interaction or at least consider other options. For instance, an experienced administrator will rarely engage an overly agitated student, since reasoning with these students could prove to be futile or even dangerous. The administrator eventually deals with these students when they restore their composure and options are considered. On the contrary, administrators often feel the need to address irate parents immediately, with no other options considered since they perceived it to be their responsibility to do so. Unfortunately, dealing with aggressive adults can result in emotional or physical harm to the school administrator. These repercussions will be examined in Chapter 5.

Notion Three: Parental Aggression Isn't an Important Issue since It Occurs Infrequently

Prior to my studies on parental aggression, I interviewed many school administrators to ascertain their attitudes regarding the topic. During these interviews, some administrators opined that episodes of parental aggression were infrequent and as a result, attention toward this issue wasn't necessarily warranted. Conversely, some administrators were of the opinion that parental aggression occurred frequently, and the issue required immediate attention. Unfortunately, both of the aforementioned observations were mere opinions involving this relatively obscure topic. Parental aggression—and the widely differing opinions regarding this issue—begged to be "researched" in order to answer the question, "How often do instances of parental aggression actually occur within our nation's schools?"

Through my two studies, I discovered that these acts of aggression occurred much more frequently than I originally suspected. At the district level, I found that approximately 71 percent of the administrators received threats by parents/guardians to contact "other authorities," that is, school board and attorneys on two or more occasions during the school year. Alarmingly, my statewide study illustrated that 79 percent of the administrators surveyed received parental threats to contact other authorities on at least three or more occasions. Chapter 10 contains additional information regarding the types and frequencies of various other forms of parental aggression.

While any type of aggression is a critical concern for school administrators, parental aggression should never be considered less dangerous or less destructive that aggression perpetrated by any other population in the scholastic setting. Does it occur to the extent for concern? I would respond with a resounding yes!

Notion Four: Instances of Parental Aggression only Seem to Happen to Me

I can help to dispel this notion by illustrating a specific statement that was included on my statewide study of parental aggression. The statement read, "My administrative colleagues have voiced their concerns regarding parental aggression." I asked the administrators to respond to this statement on a scale which ranged from strongly disagree to strongly agree. I was surprised to discover that 76 percent of the administrators agreed or strongly agreed with this statement. Administrators certainly are not alone in their encounters with aggressive parents.

Unfortunately, after these altercations, school administrators function with little emotional support, that is, debriefing, and also, they fail to request support after a conflict. Whose fault is this? Blame should not be placed with anyone, since the real reason lies within the context of Notion Four; "It only happens to me." The thinking goes, "If it only happens to me, its not worth anyone else worrying about, so its really not an issue." Understandably, it may be intimidating or unappealing for school administrators to approach their districts regarding this problem however; this may also help suppress this issue.

A practical option may be the utilization of support from colleagues at "feeder schools." Why feeder schools? One reason may be that administrators at these schools have had previous relationships with these same parents, and can offer valuable insight, advice, and support.

If feeder schools are not a viable option, school administrators could also discuss turbulent encounters with colleagues within their own schools, including fellow administrators. Optimally, a support group of sorts could be established prior to the beginning of the school year. This group could be activated after situations involving turbulent incidences, including altercations with especially taxing parents. The issue of debriefing will be discussed in more detail in Chapter 8.

An educator's time is valuable. Subsequently, formal support groups, while utilized by some administrators may not always prove to be practical. With that in mind, administrators can utilize e-mail communications or conference calls in an effort to receive or provide support. Regardless of the manner of intervention, it's imperative for school administrators to secure some type of emotional support after an altercation with a parent. This support can also be extended to individuals who were present during the altercation, that is, teachers and office personnel. In my state level study on parental aggression, I asked school administrators to respond to the statement, "I feel free discussing my experiences with hostile parents with my superiors, that is, the general director." I was pleased to discover that 86 percent of the administrators either agreed or strongly agreed with this statement. What is of the utmost importance however, is for the administrator to realize that they are not alone in their interactions with aggressive parents, and after an altercation, support should be provided if necessary.

Summary

As I continue to interact with school administrators throughout the nation, I find that these four specific notions are usually, and regrettably, maintained. Luckily, when many of these same administrators look deeper into the various aspects and facets of parental aggression, they unfailingly adopt new perspectives regarding this issue. Ironically, prior to my research I would have probably also agreed with all four of these notions. If however, I now would be asked if school administrators should be concerned about parental aggression, I would unwaveringly answer yes, it is an issue to be actively addressed and not ignored.

Tom Nelson, editor and publisher of the Campus Safety Journal states,

> The job of keeping the nation's schools safe is arguably, among the most important in the nation today. Recently, school administrators and others who are responsible for campus safety, have been

faced with a new challenge—parent versus administrator aggression. This is a growing problem in many communities, which manifests itself in different ways. While administrators have typically focused on student safety—and rightly so—recent developments have them focusing on their own safety as well. The issue of parental aggression is of critical importance and should not be ignored by school leaders.

Discussion

1. How frequently do you encounter parental aggression?

2. In your opinion, what makes dealing with aggressive parents different than any of your other duties?

3. Where do you "draw the line" when interacting with confrontational or aggressive parents?

3

Why Do Parents Become Confrontational?

If school administrators calculated their years of college, plus the years of service required before they actually achieved an administrative position, it's fairly safe to bet that there has been an investment of about of 12 to 15 years. It's also safe to bet that at some point, it was decided that educating children was a pretty valuable and worthwhile endeavor. More than anyone, administrators are aware that for many students the school provides meals, makes medical care available, provides counseling in times of distress, or provides recreational activities. If you name it, the school probably provides it, or at least will see to it that the student gets what he or she needs. Administrators are usually responsible for overseeing the majority of these services, and have a good idea what resources are available or not available for your students. All this is done in an effort to create a campus environment that fosters a safe, positive, learning atmosphere for students.

It's inevitable that some parents will not be satisfied with the school's decisions. Administrators then find themselves staring at a freight train of sorts—an angry parent. Of course most administrators act in the best interest of the child and the school, but so often they find themselves in the unenviable position of defending the school, one of their employees, or even themselves. Before we discuss how to effectively interact with unhappy parents—the same parents whose children we try our best to provide for—let's look at some factors that could contribute to parental aggression.

Simply, people get angry when they don't get what they want. Coupled with the inability to civilly secure what they want or need, unpleasant conflicts occur. Margolis (1990) explains that there are two reasons that people choose to verbally attack. The first reason is anger, and the second reason is feigned anger in an attempt to get something.

One reason anger is displayed is that the parent believes that they are being treated unfairly or are threatened, and the parent may feel helpless to rectify the situation. Margolis (1990), states, "It (anger) is an acute and often encompassing response to the presumption that unless the matters improve, they (or in the case of parents, their children) will suffer unjustly" (p. 35). Parents may also vent anger toward the school administrator since they need to emote and the administrator, who holds a position of authority, symbolizes a system by which the parent feels threatened. In addition, parents may also emote since they feel safest directing these emotions at the individual most capable of providing assistance, the school administrator.

Individuals feign anger in an attempt to manipulate the situation at hand. When successful, the behavior is reinforced, and the chances of further attempts at manipulation will increase. Recommendations are to assist individuals learn more socially acceptable ways to satiate their needs. The second recommendation is to problem-solve or negotiate the issues in a manner that firmly indicates that you will not be manipulated. Feigned anger should be addressed in a manner that fosters cooperation. The reciprocation of anger as the result of feigned anger only works to reduce the chances of an effective response Margolis (1990).

Below are several variables that may result in parental aggression. This list however, is by no means all-inclusive.

Family Violence Patterns

Have you ever addressed the behavior of a "challenging" student, and later have a meeting with their parents? After this meeting have you ever uttered the familiar phrase, "The apple sure didn't fall far from the tree, did it?" I'll bet you have. I have—about 500 times! Here is another comment I often hear, "It's hard to blame the kid for acting like that. Did you meet his father?" It is difficult to hold children responsible if their parents are considered incapable of effectively addressing even the simplest of situations, let alone more complicated matters. I think that's a reasonable perception; it makes sense!

What we at times fail to realize however, is that if the "apples don't indeed fall far from tree," then in most likelihood, that tree (the parent) started from an apple seed that fell from another tree, namely the student's grandparents. What if we had the capability of knowing the background of the individuals who so aggressively confront us? Would we interact with them differently? Not really you say, they're still attacking us! You're probably right, and this isn't the time for analyzing family trees, however, it could possibly explain why individuals act as they do. As a result, this realization could help us rationalize their aggressive actions. It's no secret that children learn patterns of violence from their parents. In much the same way, these confrontational or aggressive parents may have been predisposed to violent behavior through their own upbringing. In turn, these learned behaviors—that include aggressive resolutions of challenges or conflict—are implemented by parents when they address an undesirable situation within the school. Unfortunately, school administrators are all too often the perceived reason for these undesirable situations.

Unstable Family Environments

In 1996, the U.S. Census Bureau reported that 29.2 million (3 in 10) households were maintained by women with no husbands within the household. Nearly half of all American children will experience a portion of their childhood or adolescence being raised by a single parent. As a result of these staggering statistics, it is understandable that familial stress may result. In specific situations, this stress may manifest itself in aggression or confrontational attitudes toward school administrators.

Every day, administrators come into contact with parents and guardians who may be overwhelmed with the reality of raising children with little or no support from spouses or extended family. This lack of support and instability often results in a decrease in the student's academic and educational performance. It is conceivable that the student may be reacting to parental conflicts, however the parent may view their child's sub par school performance as another mounting problem to be dealt with. The parent demands answers from the school administrator, not realizing the actual source of the difficulties are issues within their own household.

Financial Concerns

The increase in single parent households results in more children being raised in poverty, which correlates with lower educational performance and attainment. In 1994, 19 percent of white children, 29 percent of Hispanic children, and 60 percent of black children resided in single-family households (Young and Smith, 1997).

Financial demands obviously place a great deal of stress on parents and guardians. This stress may be transferred to the school administrator for numerous reasons, including a parent's sense of inferiority stemming from possible unemployment, disability, or other financial hardship. In addition, the school is increasingly viewed as a provider of services including medical care, free/reduced meals, and so on. When these services aren't rendered (for reasons such as non-eligibility), the parent may question why they aren't provided. A simple straightforward answer may not be enough to appease a parent if they are encountering financial difficulties, and school administrators find themselves in a very challenging position.

Alienation from the School Community

When a parent is detached from the school community or makes no effort to actively participate in school activities, in a sense they have alienated themselves from the school community. Reasons for this detachment may be due to a simple lack of transportation to any number of personal reasons. This alienation prevents the parent from familiarizing themselves with school administrators and vice versa. This lack of familiarity prevents both parties from acquainting themselves with the other party and aggression may be experienced that may have otherwise been avoided. This is not to say of course, that disagreements could never occur, however conflicts with a familiar person may be of less intensity since both individuals are more aware with the style and manner of the other party.

Inaccurate Perceptions of Administrators

If parents form inaccurate, negative perceptions of the school administrator, their behaviors may in turn be based on these misperceptions. The parent, who views the school administrator as aloof, uncaring, or arrogant may be more prone to communicate with that administrator in an aggressive manner. The parent's self-esteem may also be threatened due to an inaccurate perception of the administrator as a "superior." The key word here is misperception. If a parent proceeds to inaccurately view the administrator in a negative manner, the administrator not only deals with the problem at hand, but also feelings of frustration regarding these inaccurate perceptions. A colleague of mine who is an assistant principal once told me, "parents get angry when they perceive that we (administrators) aren't listening…that we really don't hear them. That's unfortunate, plus it's a misconception, since we are listening and truly do hear them."

Previous Negative School Experiences

School administrators value education, and attempt to pass this value to the students within the scholastic environment. As unbelievable as it may seem, some parents place little value on education. One possible explanation could be the parent's own negative experiences while they attended school. For instance, as a student, the parent may have had poor academic performance, behavioral difficulties, or conflicts with school personnel, and these difficulties resulted in the parent possessing a less than favorable view of education. These negative feelings toward education surface years later, as the parent now addresses difficulties involving their children. While these difficulties may be very similar to the ones once experienced "in their day," school administrators find themselves in the position of interacting with parents with a poor overall attitude toward education.

The School Administrator's Attitude

As we will see in Chapter 4, predispositions can affect the nature of our interactions. Could it be that is not always the parent's fault? As school administrators have been confronted by aggressive parents, conversely, most school administrators have also experienced situations where their own attitudes and actions were in question, and this resulted in conflict. School administrators may indeed be a major part of the reason for the parent/administrator conflict. Reasons may include; the administrator's lack of interpersonal skills, unpleasant past dealings with the parent, the parent's personality, or the fact that the administrator may simply not be fond of the parent. Fortunately, school administrators can be offered instruction in interpersonal skills techniques that greatly reduce their chances of becoming engaged in parental conflict. Some of these techniques will be discussed in a later chapter.

Parents' Fear of Their Own Child

Many school administrators have told the story of irate parents who arrived at school, loudly and forcefully exclaiming that their son or daughter has not been given a fair chance, is constantly picked on, or is not liked by a certain teacher, and so on. Within minutes, administrator and parents are in the administrator's office, and the parents, on the verge of tears, explain that they are at a total impasse as to controlling their child's behavior. It's apparent that the student, who is posing significant difficulties within the school, is doing the same at home. The parents, initially irate when entering the school are actually reacting out of fear and frustration. The parents' anger is not actually against the school administrator, but toward their own son or daughter with whom they are loosing control.

Summary

While not an all-inclusive list, these factors are indeed main sources of parental aggression. Although the administrator can be aware of these factors, it does not make dealing with an irate parent any easier. It is however, advantageous to be aware of these sources of parental aggression since this knowledge could temper the school administrator's own stance when interacting with hostile parents. Administrators, as a result, become cognizant that the problem isn't actually with them, but rather with other issues facing parents. School administrator find themselves acting as sounding boards for parents, but only after the initial confrontational or aggressive approach by parents. Getting parents from the initial anger stage to the point where they will share the real reason for their anger is a challenge. In Chapter 4, we will examine three oversights that must be avoided, if this challenge is be overcome.

Discussion

1. During your most recent encounter with aggressive parents, to what would you attribute their anger?

2. Have you ever detected a "common denominator" in aggressive parents?

3. In your opinion, what is the most significant variable which influences parental aggression?

4

Three Issues Affecting Interactions with Confrontational Parents

While examining the topic of parental aggression, I became aware of three relatively obscure and overlooked issues that consistently work against school administrators. It is apparent that there is no real relationship among the three issues; however, overlooking these issues can sabotage any effort to remediate a turbulent encounter with a volatile parent.

The first issue is overlooking the importance of proper nonverbal communication and "physical attending skills." The second issue is administrators' lack of awareness regarding their own predisposition toward conflict. The third oversight is administrators' lack of awareness regarding unrealistic expectations that parents may have for their children.

A Lack of Awareness in
the Area of Physical Attending Skills

Human relations and interpersonal communication skills are closely associated. Listening connotes an empathetic attitude, while caring is a condition which more often than not ensures trust (Bulach, 1993). Poor human relationships constitute most of the mistakes made by school administrators (Bulach, Pickett, & Boothe, 1998). Consequently, principals who appear, or are indeed arrogant, abusive, and inattentive to other's needs, are also more likely to loose their jobs (Davis, 1997).

When we think of interpersonal skills, verbal skills are usually most identified, however, most communication is nonverbal. Interpersonal communication skills may consist heavily of attending skills, which can be described as nonverbal communication.

I often find myself not paying enough attention to my attending skills, and as a result I wonder if this affected my interview or interaction with a parent. While easy to overlook, attending skills are very critical in any interaction, and their significance is compounded exponentially when the interaction involves an aggressive or confrontational individual.

During a conversation, how often have you caught yourself slouching, crossing your legs, not making proper eye contact or folding your arms in an effort to be comfortable? What do these postures indicate to the party across from you? Boredom? Disinterest? Indifference? All are extremely destructive perceptions when interacting with aggressive parents.

Egan (1975) identified several facets of physical attending. The acronym SOLER can be easily referred to and implemented by school administrators while in the presence of an angry parent.

Squarely face the parent. This indicates, "I am available to you."

Open postures indicate that you are "open" to the parent's input.

Leaning toward the parent indicates presence, availability, and involvement.

*E*ye contact should be maintained, however avoid "staring down."

*R*elaxation says to the parent, "I am comfortable with you."

Physical attending skills are frequently overlooked, but they remain a major part of the school administrator's communicative repertoire. While much attention is placed on verbal skills,—and rightly so—nonverbal communication is indispensable. According to Suzette Hadin Elgin in her book "The Gentle Art of Self Defense at Work (2000), "Any words be they ever so flawless, can have their meaning cancelled by body language-but not vice versa. There are no words capable of canceling the meaning transmitted by body language" (p. 45).

Identifying and Acknowledging Predispositions Toward Conflict

I have met many school administrators who have readily admitted that they erred in their approach toward aggressive parents. I have not however, met administrators who actually enjoyed admitting that their disposition may have been the actual reason for the parent's aggression or confrontational manner. During interactions with aggressive parents, school administrators should be aware of possessing possible predispositions to conflict due to the significant amount of influence they possess in these situations.

Morton Deutch (1992) identifies six dimensions of conflict response. He explains that by being aware of a predisposition toward conflict, modifications can be attempted. I found these dimensions useful for administrators in their attempts to discover how their behaviors affect parents.

Conflict Avoidance–Conflict Involvement

Conflict avoidance is manifested in denial, suppression, and continual delay in facing the conflict. Also evident is a premature resolution of the problem instead of an exploration of conflicting interests and other options for resolving the issue. Conflict avoidance results in irritability, muscular tension, fatigue, and a sense of malaise. Individuals possessing a predisposition for conflict involvement display a "macho" attitude, a chip on the shoulder, or a penchant for seeking a conflict to prove that conflict is not feared. Obsessive thoughts of fights and disputes and a rehearsal of moves and countermoves between the individual and the adversary are also evident. Deutch describes a more favorable predisposition, which includes a readiness to confront conflict without seeking or be preoccupied with the conflict.

Hard–Soft

Individuals with a hard predisposition possess an aggressive, unyielding conflict response, possibly in fear of being taken advantage of. In contrast, are soft individuals who are excessively gentle, in fear of being considered hostile. They expect others to read their minds. Deutch recommends a firm support of one's own interests and openness to other's interests.

I have known very few school administrators who have possessed a "hard" predisposition and enjoyed a long tenure. On many occasions, administrators "give in" and come to a compromise with people who disagree with them. I think they call it "picking your battles." To maintain an unyielding aggressive conflict response is to invite disaster. Unyielding and aggressive administrators usually have a difficult time with the regular school population, let alone an angry or hostile parent. Conversely, school administrators who fear that image can become immobile and easily taken advantage of by aggressive parents. The solution? Administrators who are firm, fair, confident, but gentle.

Rigid–Loose

Individuals who are rigid seek to control the situation by way of rigid arrangement. This is a consequence of perceiving threat. In contrast, there are loose individuals who are opposed to any formality. I have had the opportunity (not pleasure) to work with principals who attempted to control the situation from both ends of this spectrum.

Administrators who are excessively rigid are very difficult to work with. During a conflict, their inflexibility proves to be a real detriment regarding any attempt to remediate the difficulty. At the other end of the spectrum are administrators who function with a total lack of formality. This lack of formality could be as destructive as rigidness in the sense that the parent could perceive the administrator as uncaring and uninterested about the problem at hand or simply unqualified to address the situation.

Deutch notes that optimally, an approach that contains a blend of orderliness and flexibility is more favorable than an approach that is compulsively organized or rejects orderliness.

Intellectual–Emotional

Intellectual predispositions feel no relevant emotion as thoughts are communicated. Lying underneath this calm exterior however is fear that if emotions are expressed, someone will respond destructively or cause humiliation. Deutch also warns that the absence of emotional expressiveness may communicate to the other party a lack of interest in one's own interest and in addition, nonconcern for the other party's interest.

In contrast are emotional individuals who believe that only feelings are real, and ideas and semantics are not to be taken seriously unless they are emotionally saturated. Emotionally predisposed individuals may experience difficulty mutually exploring ideas and developing solutions in a creative manner. Emotionally predisposed individuals also have difficulty distinguishing significant from insignificant. According to Deutch, the optimal mode of communication couples both thought and affect. Thought is supported by affect and affect is explained by thought.

Escalating–Minimizing

Individuals with an escalating predisposition engage in conflict in the largest of terms. These individuals perceive that the issues at stake are cast to involve one's self, family, ethnic group, and precedence for all time. Escalation of the conflict makes resolution difficult. At the other extreme are those who minimize conflict.

If administrators consistently escalate hostility with aggressive parents, I feel confident in stating that their careers are usually short lived. The burnout issue becomes a real possibility since these instances of conflict—whether with parents, student or staff—occur so frequently.

Administrators who minimize conflict are more prevalent. While minimizing conflict can work toward diffusing a turbulent situation, the administrator must take great care to not minimize the importance of the real reason why the parent is upset. One of the reasons parents become angered is the perception that administrators do not hear them. While the problem is not a major issue for the school administrator, it may be a major issue for parents, hence their emotionality.

Compulsively Revealing–
Compulsively Concealing

Compulsively revealing individuals reveal what they think and feel in addition to their fears and hostilities in irrational blunt manners. They are compelled to reveal every weakness or doubt about themselves. In contrast, are those who fail to reveal anything about themselves for fear of seriously damaging their relationships with the other party. Deutch cautions that either extreme can preclude the formation of constructive relationships. Open and honest communications are favorable, however, the consequences of what one says or does not say should be taken into account.

Unfulfilled Expectations, Parental
Aggression, and the School Administrator

As we discovered in Chapter 3, parents can become aggressive or confrontational for reasons that are easily understandable, that is, financial hardships, lack of family support, alienation from the school community, or previous unpleasant school experiences. Interestingly, another prevalent but rarely mentioned reason for parental hostility is children's failure to "live up to" their parent's expectations, which may be frequently and regrettably unrealistic. When children do not perform to expected levels, parents naturally experience feelings of frustration and anger. These emotions could be directed at school administrators, who in a sense, symbolize the school where the child is not meeting the parent's expectations. Unfortunately, school administrators become a natural target for these frustrated parents. Ironically, it's not an administrative issue, but rather a parental issue, since it is the parents' expectations that are not being met.

Brad B. is a principal at an Iowa middle school. He notes, "Some parents have a concern about the future of their child once they get out of school if they aren't performing like they feel *they* need to. A few parents have told me that they are concerned that their child may 'live in the basement' for the rest of their lives. These daily frustrations with the child spill into emotions with the school. Unfortunately, these emotions can sometimes be manifested in unpleasant ways when dealing with administrators."

Mary Frances C., an assistant principal at a Florida middle school, states, "I've observed several instances of students not fulfilling parental expectations. Many times, these expectations are unrealistic. When these expectations are not met, pointing the finger at the school is the easy answer. Unfortunately, it's not what could *I* have done to make the situation better, it's what could the *school* have done."

Many administrators have informed me that they have become more empathetic regarding a parent's anger after becoming aware of extenuating circumstances that may be the real reason for the anger. Frustration relating to the child's unfulfilled expectations could easily fit into this category; however, by no means does this excuse the parent's aggressive behavior. It does however; allow administrators to become cognizant that they may not have been the actual intended targets of the parent's aggression. Quite possibly, the administrator may have been perceived as a sounding board of sorts by the parent, who wants to express emotions, however intense these emotions may be. Once the administrator establishes that there may be other circumstances affecting the parent's behavior, the administrator can then proceed to diffuse the aggression with these facts in mind. Different approaches may also be considered in light of this awareness.

Checkley (2000) explains that parents are constantly in the process of losing their dreams regarding what their child will be and realizing whom their child is actually becoming. Subsequently, parents experience feelings of grief. However, if administrators are cognizant of these feelings, they can communicate with parents in new ways and the parent-school relationship will endure.

Summary

These three unrelated and obscure oversights: how administrators physically present themselves to parents; how administrators are aware of their own predisposition to conflict; and how administrators maintain awareness of parents' expectations for their children, are all significant variables that could determine the nature of the administrator/parent interaction. Although easy to disregard, their familiarity is invaluable to the school administrator.

Discussion

1. Can you identify other "obscure" issues that may interfere with your interactions with confrontational or aggressive parents?

2. Has your disposition ever interfered with an encounter with an aggressive parent?

3. How do you handle a parent who has unrealistic expectations for their child? When you address this issue with the parent, do they become defensive?

5

Engaging The Confrontational Parent: The RAID Approach

The steps taken prior to actual contact with an aggressive parent may be the most indispensable allies of the administrator. Simply approaching and engaging an aggressive or confrontational parent—whether they arrived announced or unannounced—is akin to pondering a swim in an alligator infested pond. While not all alligators attack humans, any sensible person would take extreme caution when in the proximity of the pond, since harm could obviously result. Likewise, school administrators should approach aggressive parents with similar caution. Forethought and preplanning prior to a meeting with aggressive parents are critical and can greatly deescalate a volatile situation. Not all problems are resolved during the actual meeting or conference with the parent, but rather prior to the meeting, before eyes are set on the parent, or the parent sets eyes on the administrator.

The choice to take into consideration several factors prior to the initial meeting with the parent could prevent unforeseen complications later in the meeting. What follows is a simple, brief, yet effective manner of engaging aggressive parents, it is called the *RAID* approach.

*R*ecognize the potential for a violent encounter.

*A*ssess your ability to deal with the parent.

*I*dentify your advantages.

*D*iffuse the parent during initial contact.

Recognizing the Potential for a Violent Encounter

When parents arrive on campus for a scheduled (or unscheduled) meeting with school administrators, front office workers or secretaries are in an advantageous position to initially gauge the emotional state of the parent. When office workers observe irate or agitated parents, simple preplanning could instruct the secretary/office worker to walk directly to the administrator's location in lieu of contacting the administrator by use of telephones/intercom. Once the administrator is aware of the presence of an aggressive parent, the secretary could be asked if the parent was: threatening? accompanied? wearing clothing to conceal a weapon? previously identified as aggressive during other school visits?

After these questions have been asked and concerns emerge, the administrator may feel that further information is necessary prior to the actual meeting with the parent. Additional information could be gleaned from available colleagues, including: fellow administrators, teachers, school resource officers, guidance counselors, and so on. The administrator may be tempted to ignore this brief fact-finding mission and engage the parent immediately, but this opportunity should not be ignored. This information could prove to be extremely valuable. In addition, this "questioning" period could also allow the parent to regain composure as while waiting for the administrator.

If the administrator is comfortable meeting with the parent after the information is gathered, the meeting could proceed. If however, the administrator feels that the parent could indeed pose a serious threat, it is recommended that the school resource officer be immediately notified. If the school does not have an assigned officer, or an assigned officer is not available, a police street unit should be summoned at once. The administrator should never attempt to conduct a meeting after a threat has been issued. It is also advisable that the administrator not come into view of the parent if a threat has been communicated. The rule of thumb is to gather information about the parent and don't proceed hastily and foolishly!

Assessing Your Ability to Deal with the Parent

I have witnessed certain school administrators encounter extreme parental aggression, diffuse the situation, and soon after, laugh about the encounter. I have witnessed school administrators experience great difficulty relating to an aggressive parent and then take quite some time to emotionally recover from the encounter. Even though it is impossible to predict what will transpire during an encounter with an aggressive individual, it is imperative for the school administrator to be aware of his or her own emotional ability to handle the situation prior to the actual meeting.

Various issues can easily influence a school administrator's ability to effectively deal with a turbulent situation. Three possible areas of interference include issues at home, at work, or with the parent.

Whether we admit it or not, issues at home are often carried to work. An argument with a spouse, a child presenting behavioral problems, unresolved grief, an obnoxious motorist, or any form of stress could result in a less than rosy workday disposition. While we try not to bring problems to work, it truly is difficult to leave them in the driveway until we arrive home in the evening. Also, within the school itself, administrators may be at odds with colleagues or students. These conflicts can certainly affect the mood and disposition of any administrator. In addition, the administrator may have previously had encounters with a parent that left a bad taste in the mouth. This bad taste may be due to the parent's personality, parenting techniques, or even the personality of the child. The administrator may also simply not be fond of the parent.

Subsequently, an encounter with an aggressive parent may occur, and your disposition, which was poor to start with, is now "a part" of the meeting. This pits an angry parent with an irritated school administrator, and that makes for a poor mix, any way you look at it. Administrators, while not immune to stressful situations that can alter their emotions, should be aware, or at least sensitive, to the fact that two individuals under emotional duress could come into conflict. Prior to contact with hostile parents, administrators should consider if any of the aforementioned issues could conceivably prevent optimal effectiveness or unfairly influence their attitude toward the confrontational or aggressive parents. Administrators may even have standing agreements with fellow administrators or secretaries to inform them if their disposition is noticeably poor, and possibly unbeknownst to them. While the poor colleague may consider this small task risky, in the long run, many problems, some possibly emanating from the administrator may be avoided. Once administrators are confident that they are emotionally capable of encountering and effectively dealing with aggressive parents, the identification of possible advantages is now explored.

Identifying Your Advantages

As we have discussed in the first two steps of the RAID approach, when an angry parent demands to meet with an administrator, the administrator's initial attempt is to recognize the potential for violence. Next the administrator assesses his or her ability to interact emotionally with the parent. Once these two steps have been considered, the decision is made to move to step three, identifying your advantages. This step provides an opportunity for the administrator to consider advantageous and practical resources that are available prior to the interaction with the parent. These simple advantages are often overlooked and can be divided into two categories, workforce advantages, and environmental advantages.

Workforce Advantages

There are several ways to diffuse or prevent parent confrontations, and colleagues can play an integral role in this diffusion. Surprisingly, a colleague's mere presence at the meeting or conference may deescalate an otherwise volatile situation. The colleagues should be made aware of concerns and the details of the situation prior to the start of the meeting. Colleagues to be considered for inclusion in the meeting could include school resource officers whose representation of the law acts as a powerful reminder against any violence considered by the angered parent. Many administrators though, would rather not summon an officer for fear of creating a martial type environment. If however, the administrator is not totally confident of the parent's ability to remain composed, police should at least be notified and requested to make their presence known.

Other invited colleagues could include fellow school administrators, guidance counselors, school social workers, or anyone else whose presence could act to deescalate possible violence. The parent may also act in a more subdued manner in the presence of multiple school personnel, due to the fact that the situation is not now viewed as a person-to-person conflict. The parent may also be fond of the other colleague whose presence could only help to calm the agitated parent.

For whatever reason, if the administrator cannot secure the services of a colleague to attend the meeting, then secretaries are considered a good option. The administrator may request that the secretary interrupt the meeting at a given point. Whether through head nod or code phrase, that is, "cancel my 3:00 appointment." The secretary could summon assistance if the parent becomes confrontational, aggressive, or is not likely to leave the premises when the meeting is concluded.

Environmental Advantages

School administrators should also consider environmental advantages. In most schools there are physical "considerations" which the administrator could utilize when interacting with aggressive parents. The venue should not be overlooked and it can be a great advantage for a school administrator. A large, well-lit, opened-draped room with two exits is optimal, this setting is not always available, especially when the parent arrives unannounced and rooms are already occupied. Nevertheless, in most situations, prior to meeting with the parent, the administrator should dictate where the meeting will be conducted. In addition, variables including the room's proximity to other school personnel and seating arrangement, that is, the administrator seated closest to the exit, should also be considered prior to the meeting with the parent. Blauvelt (2001) explains that mirrors have a relaxing effect on an angered person. He suggests placing a mirror behind the administrator's desk and inviting the person to have a seat (across from the mirror). After the administrator excuses herself for a short period, the angered individual usually observes his facial features. The parent invariably begins to change disposition, since the reflection is unflattering to say the least.

Administrators are also utilizing electronic devices for use during meetings with volatile parents. Audio taping (with the permission of the parent) could also be considered for clarity regarding what was and was not said during the meeting. Until recently, this administrative option would have been considered farfetched, however the increase of violence in our nation's schools has made the use of electronic devices even more prevalent. Examine your own office and conference room areas. Could electronic devices such as under-the-desk buzzers (to secretary/school resource officer) or intercoms be a viable option? If so, don't hesitate to consider installation. These devices can prove to be a real advantage for school administrators.

Diffusing the Parent
During your Initial Contact

After you have recognized the potential for a violent encounter, assessed your ability to handle the situation, and identified your advantages, you may or may not decide to proceed with the actual meeting with the parent. If you do indeed decide to proceed, the fourth and final step of the RAID model focuses on the administrator's initial contact with the parent. This brief introduction period, maybe 30 to 60 seconds in length can help to "diffuse" the angry parent and allow the subsequent meeting to occur with far less tension.

Extensive approaches exist on the topic of engaging volatile individuals; however for many of these methods it seems that graduate coursework in counseling is necessary. In addition, the initial contact with the parent is a very bad time to attempt to mentally review a 15-step approach to better communication.

I would like to identify and discuss several overlooked behaviors that may prove to be invaluable when initially contacting the hostile parent at school. They are the way an administrator walks, makes eye contact, maintains facial expression, greets, and invites the parent to discuss the problem.

The Administrator's Walk

Sometimes a person's walk says it all. A slouched, slow-paced gait is rarely impressive. Conversely, a confident, brisk, enthusiastic walk is usually indicative of an individual who is self-assured and unafraid. This is important since the administrator's initial impression may go a long way toward determining the parents' willingness to confront the administrator in an aggressive manner. It's true, while easily overlooked, the gait can say a lot about the administrator.

The Administrator's Eye Contact

The administrator's first contact with an angry parent is not a handshake or greeting. It is the initial eye contact with the parent; whether from across a spacious office at a distance of forty feet or eight feet as you turn the corner in a small, compact, office space. Good eye contact translates to sincerity and concern. During the initial contact with the parent, the administrator must relay this sincerity and concern, especially since these parents often feel that the school is against them or their child. The administrator must also convey a sense of confidence and being in control.

Good eye contact also provides an opportunity for the administrator to observe the parent and gather information regarding body language. Several body language indicators may include whether the parent appears tense or relaxed, standing at attention, or sitting in a nonchalant manner as you approach.

Keen observation also allows the administrator to assess whether individuals accompanying the parent may also be angered. In addition, eye contact allows the administrator to observe the parent for concealed weapons, although this is would obviously be an immediate signal for the administrator to postpone the meeting and contact the nearest school resource officer or police street unit.

The Administrator's Facial Expressions

It can be extremely awkward and difficult to attempt to be pleasant to someone who may want your job terminated. Although easier said than done, try to smile at the time of initial engagement, no matter the situation. A simple smile may convey to the parent that an adversary is not about to descend upon them. An angry person usually experiences difficulty confronting a person who is pleasant compared to an individual who is as angry or unpleasant. It takes at least two individuals to create a conflict, but a pleasant individual is much more difficult to engage. As tempting as it may be, a smirk is not a smile. The parent could also interpret a smirk as a flippant gesture.

Greeting the Parent

Administrators should always greet the parent by name. Neglecting this small task could indicate that the parent is not important—just another parent with a gripe. Next, by thanking the parent for coming to the school (whether scheduled or unscheduled), the administrator conveys that the arrival and concern of the parent was not dreaded, but actually welcomed. The parent subsequently senses that the meeting is also important to the administrator.

Next, the administrator asks the parent "How are you?" or reflects on the parents anger if it is obvious. While this may seen like an invitation for an explosion, it may actually be an opportunity for the administrator to observe and assess the parent's emotional state. This is advantageous since the parent's initial opportunity to communicate is immediate, not after the meeting has commenced. The parent, in a sense, is allowed to immediately begin "blowing off steam." Conversely, the administrator is also afforded an opportunity to gauge how much steam the parent actually has to "blow off."

Inviting the Parent to the Meeting

After greeting the parent, the administrator extends an invitation for the parent to join him in a prearranged room for an actual meeting to discuss the problem. The room may be a conference room or the administrator's own office. If the administrator has already decided that other school personnel will also attend the meeting, the parent should be told this prior to the meeting. This should be done in order for the parent to avoid becoming angered over feeling "set up" by the administrator.

These five simple displays; the administrator's walk, eye contact, facial expression, greeting, and invitation, may not totally diffuse the parent's anger, but displaying these behaviors could easily improve the administrator's chances of making a positive initial impression on the parent. These initial impressions often dictate the nature and tone of the subsequent meeting. If, however, parents refuse or are unable to effectively contain or control their anger and threats continue, the administrator could make an ultimatum of sorts. For example, "Mr. Jones, if you continue to make threatening remarks toward me (or other personnel) this meeting will not be possible." The school administrator should not continue with the meeting or conference if feeling threatened in any way by the parent.

To summarize, the RAID approach focuses on four simple yet effective steps to implement when encountering an angered parent. The RAID approach may initially interfere with the administrator's tendency to immediately engage the parent, but herein lies the major benefit of the RAID approach. By implementing four brief steps prior to the meeting with the parent, the RAID approach may help to eliminate factors that could negatively affect the subsequent encounter with the parent. In conclusion, when notified of an angry or volatile parent, the RAID approach invites the school administrator to

1. Realize the potential for a violent encounter.
2. Assess their ability to deal with the parent.
3. Identify their advantages.
4. Diffuse the parent's hostility through initial contact.

A leadership position requires confidence, self- assuredness, and the desire and skill to ameliorate a variety of turbulent situations. This is especially important since school administrators are in constant view of school personnel, students, parents, and the community. Positive impressions are indeed necessary and advantageous, but herein lies a danger. The administrative position and its inherent "authoritative expectations," should never preclude a safe, and prudent approach to engaging aggressive parents. The RAID model provides a simple strategy for formulating a means to an effective and preventative approach for interacting with confrontational or aggressive parents prior to the actual meeting or conference. Unnecessary difficulties may fortunately be avoided that would otherwise hinder the school administrator's effectiveness in his/her dealings with an angered parent.

Discussion

1. In your opinion, how practical is the RAID approach?

2. As an administrator, are you inclined to immediately engage an aggressive parent. If so, why do you feel that is your tendency?

3. Could the RAID approach have proved beneficial during your most recent encounter with an aggressive parent?

6

Applying The RAID Approach

Depending on the volatility of the parent, the implementation of all four steps in the RAID approach may not be necessary. To summarize, the four steps of the RAID approach are:

Step One: **R**ecognizing the potential for a violent encounter

Step Two: **A**ssessing your ability to deal with these encounters

Step Three: **I**dentifying your advantages

Step Four: **D**iffusing the parent through initial contact

To demonstrate the application of the RAID approach, several vignettes will be presented. The following four vignettes will progress from interactions with mildly aggravated parents to encounters with physically aggressive parents.

The Perturbed Parent

The school secretary informs the principal that a parent has arrived unannounced and is demanding an immediate meeting to discuss her son's grade in math. The principal remains in his office, then proceeds to Step One and assesses the potential for a violent encounter:

Principal to secretary:	"Does Mrs. Taylor appear to be aggressive or hostile in any way?"
Secretary:	"Well, she seems very irritated, but she doesn't appear to be violent."
Principal:	"Have you ever known her to be violent or overly aggressive?"
Secretary:	"No, not at all. As a matter of fact she has always been fairly pleasant when I've dealt with her."

Comment: The principal has initially asked his secretary if the parent appears to be violent. After being informed that the parent is not violent, the administrator decides to proceed with a meeting without gleaning further information about the parent. The administrator skips to Step Four feeling emotionally capable of dealing with the parent (Step Two) and does not feel that it is necessary to identify advantages for use during the meeting (Step Three). The administrator now attempts to diffuse the parent's small degree of anger, through initial contact (Step Four).

As the Principal walks enthusiastically to the front office, he makes immediate eye contact with Mrs. Taylor. He observes that the parent appears to be tense but nonthreatening. Smiling, the principal offers his hand and proceeds.

Principal:	"Hello Mrs. Taylor. Thanks so much for coming in. How have you been?"

Mrs. Taylor:	"I can't lie. I have been better. My son is really getting the bad end of a deal with one of your math teachers. I'm not happy about this. I want to talk to you now!"
Principal:	"You seem pretty upset about this."
Mrs. Taylor:	"Well, you are right. I am mad. It's my child we're talking about here! He's going to college next year and a D in math could really complicate things.
Principal:	"I understand. Could we go to my office and talk about this?"
Mrs. Taylor:	"That's fine with me."

Comment: The administrator has greeted the parent by name and thanks the parent for coming in. The administrator also reflects on the parent's emotional state, and permits the parent to display a small amount of anger. Next, the administrator invites the parent to discuss the problem at hand in a prearranged location. The meeting can now proceed with the parent fully aware that the principal is concerned and willing to correct or clarify the problem concerning her son. Conversely, the principal can proceed sensing that the parent, while obviously perturbed, is capable of addressing the situation without an overt display of aggression.

The Parent Who Makes Verbal Threats

A student is slightly injured in physical education class. His parents have been at odds previously with school personnel for a variety of reasons. The father arrives at school for a scheduled appointment. In the presence of front office personnel, he proceeds to make several verbal threats and accusations toward the physical education teacher. He demands an immediate meeting with the teacher prior to the meeting with the assistant principal. The assistant principal, who has recently suffered the loss of a close colleague at another school, is notified of the father's arrival by the secretary.

After being informed of the father's action, the assistant principal quickly assesses that the potential for a violent encounter indeed exists (Step One). Although the administrator is slightly acquainted with the father, the school resource officer is immediately summoned to the assistant principal's office. The officer provides new information to the administrator indicating that the parent has previously been confrontational and aggressive toward administrators at an adjacent elementary school where a younger son attends. On one occasion, a trespassing summons was considered against the father due to belligerent behavior.

Using Step Two, the assistant principal assesses his ability to interact with the angered parent in light of the recent loss of his colleague. While admitting to emotional fatigue, the administrator decides to proceed with the meeting.

The administrator realizes that Step Three is crucial to the success of the meeting and identifies several advantages that include requesting that the resource officer remain in the vicinity of the front office and conference room where the meeting will be conducted. The presence of the officer is intended to deter further aggression by the father. The administrator also asks the secretary to interrupt the meeting and by way of a code statement, "Should I cancel your next meeting?," ("Yes" or "No" response) possibly summon the officer to the meeting if the father's behavior necessitates intervention. In addition, the assistant principal refuses to arrange for the physical education teacher to attend the meeting, until the father's level of anger is gauged and possibly reduced. Finally, the administrator asks another assistant principal to also attend the meeting.

The administrator begins Step Four, by walking confidently to the front office and attempting to engage the parent. As the administrator approaches and makes eye contact, he notices that the parent refuses both eye contact and a handshake. The father is also now accompanied by his wife who also seems to be irritated. The following discussion transpires:

Assistant Principal:	"Hello Mr. and Mrs. Smith. Thanks for coming in."
Mr. Smith:	"I'm not here for niceties."
Assistant Principal:	"I have been informed of your son's injury."
Mr. Smith:	"He isn't the only one who's going to be hurt. I'll sue the school board and make sure you are out of here!"
Assistant Principal:	"Mr. Smith, I can see that you are really upset. Maybe we can talk about it. Another administrator is also going to join us."
Mr. Smith:	"Why another administrator? Are you afraid of me or something? Don't worry about me, worry about my attorney!"
Assistant Principal:	"My goal is to help us clarify the situation with your son. I'm really here to help you. I must inform you though, that if any further threats are made, this meeting will end immediately. I really hope we don't need to do that."
Mr. Smith:	"Whatever! Lets get this meeting started because I've got a lot to say."

Comment: In Step Four, the administrator greeted the parent, and reflected on the parent's disposition in an attempt to gauge the level of parental aggression by stating, "You seem really upset." The administrator immediately detects a significant degree of hostility. After the parent continues to make threatening legal statements against the administrator, the assistant principal firmly informs the parents that further threats could jeopardize the meeting. Ground rules have now been established. With these strategies in place a meeting with the parent can begin in an attempt to rectify the situation.

The Physically Aggressive Parent

A school bus containing an eighth-grade class has returned to the campus after a field trip to a local zoo. Immediately after the bus arrives, the father of one of the students enters the school and demands an immediate conference with the principal. The secretary asks for the purpose of the request and the father explains irately, that his daughter telephoned him from the zoo and explained that one of the field trip chaperones asked her, "What kind of parents would raise a behavior problem like you?"

The administrator has been made aware of the chaperone's comment from a telephone call from another chaperone earlier in the day when the student was observed to be very upset and subsequently questioned. The secretary informs the principal of the father's arrival, and is questioned regarding the father's disposition. The secretary explains that the father, a very imposing man, made a statement to the effect, "I'll show them what kind of parent raises a behavior problem like that!"

Using Step One, the principal recognizes the potential for a violent encounter. Further information is considered necessary, and the student's assistant principal is summoned. The administrator informs the principal that the child has extensive behavioral referrals and conferences with the father have been tense at best. The school resource officer is summoned and proceeds to inform the principal that the father has an extensive history of violence and has little respect for authority figures.

The principal considers herself emotionally capable of dealing with the father (Step Two) and now decides to identify advantages before the meeting is conducted (Step Three). The principal elects to have the school resource officer actually attend the meeting. The principal also decides to have the chaperone attend the meeting, however the arrival of the chaperone at the meeting is intentionally delayed until the parent's anger is gauged.

The principal proceeds to the front office to meet the parent (Step Four). The officer follows behind at a distance, but well within view of the parent. As the principal approaches, the parent asks:

Parent:	"What kind of idiots do you send on field trips to watch our kids?"
Principal:	"Hello Mr. Kramer, thanks for coming in. I've been informed about the incident on the field trip."
Parent:	"Are you going to do something about it or am I?"
Principal:	"I know you are upset, but we can discuss it. Are you OK with that?"
Parent:	"Somebody insults me and my kid and I'm suppose to be fine with it? I think somebody is going to answer for this. Where is this chaperone? Why is this cop here?"
Principal:	"Officer Ferguson was asked to attend this meeting at my request."
Parent:	"What is he going to do, pepper spray me? I've had it done to me before and I really don't care anymore!"
Principal:	"Mr. Kramer, I don't think a meeting now is going to be a good idea. Maybe we can meet when you are a little less upset."
Parent:	"You and your school are a bunch of morons." (Parent knocks over a chair and directs vulgarity toward the principal. He then shoves the principal. The parent is subsequently arrested for disorderly conduct).

Comment: The principal, by recognizing a potential for a violent encounter in Step One, makes a wise choice by having the school resource officer present from the onset of contact with the father. Upon initial contact with the parent, the father's confrontational disposition is apparent. As the father makes the first of several comments that result in the principal questioning the father's emotional stability, the decision is immediately made to not proceed with a meeting. The principal fortunately realizes that this matter could be more adequately handled by law enforcement.

The Parent Who Unexpectedly Becomes Aggressive

A mother telephones the principal and requests a conference to discuss a possible teacher change for her fourth grade son. When asked about the reason for this request, the parent blatantly refuses to discuss the matter until the conference is conducted. Later in the day, the secretary informs the principal that the mother has arrived and is accompanied by her ex-husband. The secretary explains that the mother is calm, but the father appears to be slightly inebriated.

The principal assesses that there is a remote chance that the situation could become volatile, due to the father's possible inebriation (Step One). All other "precontact" inquiries with school personnel conclude that the child is a good student not considered a behavioral problem. The mother is also not known as aggressive. The father is an unknown figure however, due to his residence in another state.

The principal considers himself capable of intervening in the situation (Step Two). The principal identifies several advantages (Step Three) including having the secretary interrupt the meeting at a specified point to inquire as to the status of another fictitious meeting. A positive response could indicate a problem (i.e., "Yes Mrs. Jones, the meeting is still on."). At this point support could be sought for the principal. Another advantage is having the drapes opened for outside view of the meeting. The principal also alerts the assistant principal to remain in the proximity of the meeting since no school resource officer is available. In addition, the principal requests "coverage" for the student's teacher in case her presence is necessary at any time during the meeting.

The principal begins Step Four by going to the front office to greet the parents. The principal approaches the parents and notices the mother makes limited eye contact. The father is a large, intimidating person and stares as the principal approaches. The principal verbally greets both and offers his hand. The mother weakly engages in a handshake, but the father refuses the handshake altogether. The principal thanks the parents for coming to the school and does not detect alcohol on the father. The parents are directed to a conference room for the meeting. Both remain silent and follow the principal:

Principal:	"Again, thank you for coming to school to discuss this matter."
Mother:	"Thanks for having us in, but to be frank, his father has some concerns regarding Georgie's academic performance."
Principal:	"I'm confused. Georgie does well academically. Everyone speaks highly of him."
Mother:	"But he is only making B's and he even made a C last semester!"
Principal:	"Do you feel he could do better?"
Mother:	"Truthfully, I'm OK with it, but his father here is livid about his performance. He wants straight A's and nothing else will do. Ask him yourself."
Principal:	"Mr. Hammond, you feel that Georgie could do better?"
Father:	"Isn't that what she just said? Aren't you listening?"

Principal:	"You seem angry Mr. Hammond. Can we discuss this matter?"
Father:	(Exploding and pounding his fist on the table). "Listen, you probably set low standards for yourself, but I don't. I won't accept anything but straight A's. I don't care if I do live in another city, I'm involved in my kids education. Do you have a problem with that?"
Secretary:	(Hears father yelling and enters meeting) "Mr. Bellows, Is your three o'clock meeting still on?"
Principal:	"Yes Mrs. Jones, it is still on." (Secretary immediately summons the assistant principal.)

The assistant principal walks to the conference room and observes the father pointing at the principal in a threatening manner. The assistant principal walks into the meeting and requests to see the principal outside of the room. As the principal attempts to leave the room, the father makes verbal threats toward the principal. The father rises from his chair with the principal, but the mother grabs him and pulls him down into his chair. The father continues to use profanity and the odor of alcohol is now detected. Once outside of the room, both administrators agree to contact the police.

While the administrators are out of the room, the mother urges the father to leave the school. The parents exit the school, but not before the father shouts expletives in the presence of office staff and several students.

Comment: By initially assessing the situation and suspecting a slight possibility for problems, the principal made the proper decision to explore all of his advantages. The secretary intervened with the predetermined "alert response" that indicated trouble was imminent. The assistant principal was also ready to intervene when necessary. In addition, the "openness" of the room enabled the assistant principal to view the proceedings immediately. All of these advantages were implemented during this unexpected conflict.

Discussion

1. How many times in the past two years have you encountered a parent whom you considered verbally
threatening or physically aggressive? Have you ever
encountered a parent who unexpectedly became aggressive?

2. Has there been an instance when you were at a impasse as to how to deal with an aggressive or confrontational parent? If so, how did you handle this situation?

3. Is there a step in the RAID approach that you find most
valuable? Is there a step that you find difficult or uncomfortable to apply?

7

Conducting and Terminating Meetings with Confrontational Parents

As discussed in Chapter 6, approaching aggressive or confrontational parents should be done with caution. The RAID Approach offers a practical approach to initially engaging these parents, since the first minutes of contact with an aggressive parent can escalate or deescalate their anger.

It's very important to realize however, that although the parent could be "diffused" during the initial engagement, their anger could easily re-erupt. Subsequently, it is the responsibility of the school administrator to give the angered parent little opportunity to reescalate aggression during the subsequent meeting.

Although I strongly ascribe to the preplanned RAID approach, I am more eclectic in my approaches when actually interacting with confrontational or aggressive parents. Hundreds of articles and books have been written on suggestions and warnings regarding techniques for implementation during meetings with volatile individuals. With that in mind, I will attempt to illustrate my favorite, practical techniques as a guide for school administrators. By identifying various techniques, school administrators will have an opportunity to consider new or modified approaches to be used when meeting with aggressive or confrontational parents.

I Gotta Be Me

In my opinion, there is one quality that remains preeminent in the school administrator's arsenal of communication skills. It is the ability to be perceived as genuine. Genuineness does not lend itself to practice. According to Egan (1976), "genuineness is a set of attitudes and behaviors that modify the entire communication process" (p.146). Egan also offers a checklist of behaviors that relate to genuineness. The value of this checklist lies in your willingness to assess your level of genuineness in "overall terms." Weak areas or strong areas can be identified and addressed if necessary. Ask yourself the following questions:

- ♦ Are you your natural self? Is your language your own or is it stilted?
- ♦ Are you spontaneous (yet tactful) or is there something rigid and planned about your interactions?
- ♦ Do you avoid defensiveness? How do you handle negative confrontations?
- ♦ Are you open? Do you share yourself willingly and appropriately?
- ♦ Do you express what you think and feel, without putting a number of filters between you and others?
- ♦ Is your behavior generally consistent or are you one person at one time and another person later? Are you consistent yet spontaneous?
- ♦ Do you play games? Do you try to control or manipulate others?

Very few of us can positively answer every question on this checklist. For example, I usually consider my communication "open," however, when I am attacked, I tend to become defensive. Truthfully, I don't believe that this makes me a nongenuine person, but it is an area of which I should be aware, especially if this defensiveness interferes with my ability to relate to an aggressive parent.

What the Pros Say

Four authors and their approaches to dealing with difficult individuals follow. As you examine these lists, pick and choose techniques that appeal to you. Also, be cognizant of the "don'ts" when interacting with aggressive or confrontational individuals.

Muriel Solomon (1990) in her book, "Working with Difficult People"(pp. 284–285), presents several guidelines that can assist individuals when dealing with troublesome individuals.

- *Put the problem people in proper perspective.* You may just be an obstacle or essential ingredient to the person actually getting what they want.

- *Take your pick—positive or negative.* If you cling to negative feelings, you can't concentrate on constructive alternatives. Vent your emotions and cool off.

- *Don't expect difficult people to change.* They won't, but you could change the outcome by choosing a better approach.

- *Learn to respond as well as listen.* Express your emotions. Instead of making accusations, ask questions. By permitting others to save face, you give them room to change their minds.

- *Give and request frequent feedback.* Let emotional people vent their feelings before you try to reason with them and explore options. Use open-ended questions.

- *Look first at policies and procedures.* The disagreement is then begun on a high professional level. Don't place blame unless you made the mistake, for which you apologize immediately and then move on.
- *Deal directly and discreetly.*
- *Document for self-protection.*
- *Be straightforward and unemotional.*
- *Be gracious.*

Elaine McEwan in her book "How to deal with Parents Who Are Angry, Troubled, Afraid, or Just Plain Crazy (1998), provides the following "do's and don'ts" when interacting with upset parents (p. 25–38).

Things to Do

- Shake hands and welcome parents.
- Sit eye-to-eye and knee-to-knee.
- Listen.
- Open your mind.
- Establish time limits.
- Apologize.
- Get to the point.
- Empathize.
- Ask questions.
- Speak gently and say the right things.
- Redirect.
- Lower the boom (negative news) lightly.
- Welcome constructive criticism.
- Consider cultural differences in communication.
- Take your time.
- Don't tell them; show them.
- Don't fight 'em; join 'em (enlist the parents' help).
- Give options to parents.
- Focus on the problem not the personalities.

Things Not to Do

- ◆ Don't interrupt.
- ◆ Don't try to change the subject.
- ◆ Never focus on things that can't be changed.
- ◆ Don't start complaining about your own agenda.
- ◆ Don't engage in silent combat.
- ◆ Don't start rehearsing your answer before you've actually heard what the parent is trying to communicate.
- ◆ Don't advise unless asked.
- ◆ Don't persuade a parent that you are right and they are wrong.
- ◆ Don't try so hard to be neutral and show no empathy.
- ◆ Don't come across as a "know it all" professional.
- ◆ Don't talk compulsively and over-explain.
- ◆ Don't let yourself get backed into a corner.
- ◆ Don't be so intent on smoothing a conflict that you achieve a superficial solution.

Richard Rucci (1990) provides the following do's and don'ts in his paper "Dealing with Difficult People: A Guide for Educators" (pp. 77–78):

- ◆ Remain calm and cool.
- ◆ Listen, listen, listen.
- ◆ Low but firm assertive voice.
- ◆ Don't patronize.
- ◆ Don't intimidate.
- ◆ Use a friendly reassuring greeting.
- ◆ Repeat or reframe the concern.
- ◆ Discuss negotiate and compromise only when both sides are calm.
- ◆ Don't be afraid to seek assistance.
- ◆ Don't blow your top!

Principals Mary Ann Chapko and Marian Buchko, in their article "Surviving the Principalship"(2001), offer the following suggestions for school administrators:

- Maintain a sense of humor.
- Grow thicker skin to deflect the comments that will be hurled at you.
- Try not to take the negative stuff personally.
- Realize that it is impossible to please everyone; no matter how hard you try.
- Regard parents as your greatest potential allies.

I shared some of these lists and suggestions with my administrative colleagues and their feedback is favorable to say the least. I am confident that the majority of school administrators actively utilize the techniques on the preceding lists. The lists' real value however, may lie in the possible discovery of a specific technique(s) that may not be included in an administrator's current repertoire. By utilizing a new technique or avoiding a pitfall, interactions with aggressive parents can become more productive and less troublesome for the school administrator.

Some Additional Tips

I find the following techniques especially effective during meetings and conferences with confrontational or aggressive parents. If you are not familiar these techniques, you may want to consider implementing them, since they may prove effective during a turbulent meeting or conference.

- *Observe the parent's verbal and nonverbal body language.* In Chapter 4, we examined the importance of proper attending skills , that is, our nonverbal behavior. It really does make a significant difference during our interactions with aggressive parents. Just as parents observe nonverbal behavior, school administrators should observe the angered parent's verbal and nonverbal behavior. Rucci (1991) explains that educators should observe rate of speech, sentence structure and clarity, articulation, tone, and voice volume. Rucci also considers nonverbal behavior equally as important. For example, eye contact, positioning, gestures, and facial expressions all are to be considered when interacting with a difficult person.

♦ *Thank the parent(s) again for bringing the issue to your attention.* It's a simple but powerful thing to do even though you have already thanked the parent for their arrival (See the RAID approach in Chapter 5). By once again extending thanks for the parent's concern as you begin the meeting, you convey to the parent that as a school administrator, the issue is important. If parents perceive their concerns as legitimate, this could go a long way toward deescalating irritation or anger.

♦ *Empower the parent by asking for a favor.* It seems like a strange option, especially since it is difficult at best to request a favor from an angry person, however a parent's anger may, for whatever reason, stem from feelings of hopelessness. By asking for a "favor," the parent now actively participates in the problem's solution. For example, during the meeting, the administrator may ask, "Mrs. Taylor, you mentioned that Jason really reacts well when asked to read from his personal reading material at home. Could you please see to it that his teacher has a couple of those books for his leisure reading time in class?" Another example: "Mr. Jones, I know that you are upset regarding the lack of after school monitors on the basketball courts. We are looking for additional adult monitors. Could you volunteer for an hour or two a week?"

♦ *Don't overwhelm the parent with educational jargon.* Nothing turns off or irritates a parent more than being overwhelmed by an administrator who employs excessive educational jargon. It happens more than you think. Parents may perceive this as a threat or even an indication that they are unknowledgeable and incapable of participating in the resolution of the problem.

♦ *Attempt to end the meeting on a high note.* You may not feel like making the best of a very turbulent situation, but it just may be the most prudent thing to do. Chances are, you will have contact with the parent(s) in the near future, and the upbeat manner in which the last meeting ended may be remembered. Try to summarize the positives that resulted from the meeting and attempt to instill hope that the problem can indeed be resolved. Use humor (if appropriate) and smile!

♦ *Walk the parent to the front office or exit at the conclusion of the meeting.* This conveys to the parent that your time wasn't "forced," and you were not in a hurry to rid yourself of them (even though in reality you may have indeed been eager for them to leave!). Escorting the parent also serves to make sure that they don't attempt to engage other school personnel in further acts of aggression, for example, use of inappropriate language.

♦ *Make a follow up contact with the parent.* A short follow-up telephone call or note indicating your appreciation for the meeting goes a long way toward ensuring that the parent that you sincerely care about their problem. The parent may approach you with more trust and less anger in the future.

♦ *Do what you promised.* This is critical, since failure to deliver what was promised, indicates to the parent that their concern was not legitimate or important enough to warrant attention in the first place. In addition, it also makes the administrator look "nongenuine." Consequently, in an effort to receive satisfaction, the parent may now attempt to "move up the ladder" to a school board or legal level in an attempt to resolve their problem or concern.

Obviously, it is impractical to memorize every suggestion or bit of advice listed above. By reviewing these suggestions you may however, identify areas which tend to sabotage your efforts to constructively interact with hostile parents. I've reviewed these "do's and don'ts" on many occasions and discovered several areas, which necessitated attention. For example, I tend to overlook documentation and lend conversations to memory. I have also occasionally failed to establish time limits and then proceed to wonder why meetings are too lengthy. In addition, I can be too verbose and when criticism is directed at me, I tend to take it seriously. Throughout my career, I've become aware of these do's and don'ts, and made efforts to implement or avoid them.

Discussion

1. As outlined in this chapter, what suggestions or recommendations are in your current repertoire for dealing with confrontational or aggressive parents? Are there any new suggestions that you find useful?

2. If you were asked to give a future administrator three suggestions for interacting with confrontational or aggressive parents, what would they be?

3. Do you ever engage in "don'ts" that tend to sabotage interactions with confrontational or aggressive parents?

8

The Effects of Parental Aggression and Debriefing

While conducting presentations on parental aggression throughout the country, school administrators more than willingly describe their involvement in altercations with confrontational or aggressive parents. I make it a point to ask these administrators, that if in their opinion, any ramifications could result from these situations. Not surprisingly, administrators consistently identify stress as the major result of encounters with aggressive parents. Unfortunately, many administrators also overlook this important issue and offer a variety of reasons for ignoring the negative effects of these volatile encounters. I've heard rationalizations including "Stress is part of my job," "I don't have time to get upset," "Parents don't scare me," and "I wouldn't give them the satisfaction of upsetting me."

Although stress can emanate from any situation, parental conflicts may distinguish themselves in the sense that angered adults, for example, are capable of retaliating in ways that are unavailable, say, to the student population. For instance, an adult has at their disposal, the capability to pursue recourse from school boards, attorneys, or administrative superiors if their displeasure or anger is not abated.

Stress must be recognized and dealt with since it can easily interfere with a consistent administrative performance. Whether, simply unaware or intentionally ignoring the affects of stress, school administrators could expose themselves to a wide variety of difficulties. Conversely, by becoming aware of the effects of stress, an assortment of difficulties could be prevented or at least drastically reduced.

Benjamin (1987) makes several interesting generalizations regarding stress:

♦ What may be distressful to one individual may be positively stressful to another.

♦ Whether an event causes distress is dependent on the individual's perception of the situation.

♦ How a person responds to stress depends on the environment, the magnitude of the stressor, what has transpired previously, and the individual's self-perceived ability to handle the stressor, the person's physical condition, and habit.

♦ Stress can be self-imposed or situational.

♦ Type A individuals are more prone to stress reactions than those who are able to take themselves less seriously than their counterparts.

What follows is a brief look at the various symptoms of stress that a school administrator may experience as a result of interactions with confrontational or aggressive parents.

Cognitive Effects of Stress

According to Mitchell and Everly (1995), the cognitive symptoms of excessive stress include confused thinking, difficulty with decision-making, lowered concentration, memory dysfunction, and lowering of higher cognitive functioning. Obviously, all of these functions are necessary for the administrator to fully and effectively function during the course of a routine school day. After an encounter with an aggressive parent, the administrator must be aware of the possibility of any of these cognitions being negatively affected.

Emotional Effects of Stress

Emotional symptoms of excessive stress may include shock, anger, depression, or feelings of being overwhelmed. Are these feelings normal? In most cases, they are. In much the same way that any individual could be traumatized when verbally or physically accosted in public, school administrators can likewise be emotionally traumatized after a confrontation with an aggressive parent.

Joe B., a middle school assistant principal explained, "I have a duty to communicate with parents, however these 'communications' can lead to the parent becoming angered. Usually, I am confident that I will effectively deal with angry parents, but there is a difference between anger and hostility. Hostile parents have threatened me with job termination, suits or physical harm. I refuse to deal with parents who act this way. I expect anger occasionally, but hostility eats away at me."

As a result of stressful encounters with parents, time and assistance must be afforded to the administrator's emotional recovery. This will be addressed later in this chapter.

Physical Affects of Stress

Much has been written regarding the physical symptoms of excessive stress. Chances are, most school administrators probably claim that they alone could author a chapter or two on this topic. I've observed that school administrators who handle stress most effectively have plans for handling stress before it occurs, that is, exercise, relying on strong peer networks, and scheduled vacations.

When I conducted a statewide study of parental aggression toward school administrators, I decided to include a question that related to the physical affects of stress as the result of parental aggression. Among the health related issues identified by administrators: stomach distress, insomnia, irritable bowel difficulties, high blood pressure, cracked teeth from grinding during sleep, chest pains, anxiety attacks, depression, and headaches.

One middle school principal noted, "After an incident in 1999, doctors prescribed me antidepressants for stress. I brought a lawsuit against a parent for making false statements to the media."

Another middle school principal commented, "I dealt with the parent of an Exceptional Education student who was so hostile, that I began to lose sleep. I suffered a 'frozen shoulder' that spring that I think was caused by me tensing up all night."

While it remains the administrator's duty to interact with parents, administrators should however, be aware that these encounters could result in health related difficulties. Conversely, it also the responsibility of their school districts to be cognizant of the deleterious effects of these encounters.

Social and Behavioral Effects of Stress

After an interaction with an aggressive parent, for the remainder of the day, the school administrator is faced with the challenge of continuing to interact with a multitude of students, colleagues, school personnel, or even other parents. These interactions must be professional and pleasant since, of course, these individuals had nothing to do with the confrontation with the parent.

While the parent can simply leave campus and engage in whatever activity necessary to decrease their level of stress, the school administrator is rarely afforded this luxury. Understandably, after an altercation with an angry parent, school administrators may become sensitive to criticism, opposing viewpoints, or suggestions. According to Mitchell and Everly (1995), the behavioral symptoms of excessive stress could include changes in eating, withdrawal from others, and prolonged silences. As the administrator continues to interact during the remainder of the school day, an "awareness" must be maintained regarding the amount of patience, fairness, and tolerance exhibited in light of the previous confrontation. In addition to these school based social considerations, school administrators must be aware of the effects on their family relationships. Although difficult, administrators must not let the prior confrontation affect the quality of interaction with others. It simply would not be fair to the uninvolved party.

One middle school assistant principal commented, "When I have an unpleasant encounter with an unreasonable parent, the confrontation creates a rush that upsets my entire system. I constantly think about the situation, I replay it, and I plan for future confrontations. My relationships with my wife and kids begin to suffer, all because I am focused on the situation rather than on them."

The Value of Debriefing

As a member of a district crisis intervention team, I have seen many individuals fail to take the opportunity to discuss and reflect on their involvement in the day's stressful events. This is called debriefing. There is any number of reasons for an administrator's refusal to debrief following a conflict. Reasons include: not enough time, no qualified individuals to conduct the debriefing, or not ready to discuss the event. For some individuals, debriefing is unwelcome and they attempt to operate as usual. For others, turbulent events result in an emotional disequilibrium of sorts that render them temporarily ineffective. I've seen very few administrators emerge from an altercation with a volatile parent and easily and effectively resume their daily duties. Every administrator should have the opportunity to debrief.

Some schools install teams that function to debrief school personnel after an emotionally laden incident. Don W. is an assistant principal in a large California Senior High School. He explained, "At our school, the 'administration team' always debriefs any volatile situation. This allows us to discuss any options that could have been used to diffuse what occurred. It also lets us discuss how we can proact to avoid future problems."

The presence of a school-based debriefing team is optimal, however this option is not always available. Informal debriefings could be more practical since they consist of simply talking to a colleague including fellow principals or assistant principals. Many administrators contact colleagues at other schools and share their experiences.

Administrators who are fortunate enough to share good communicative relationships with their superiors often call them immediately following a conflict. This serves to both emotionally debrief and also make the administrator's case clear if the parent decides to themselves contact the superiors regarding the incident.

According to Myrna R. a general director in a large Florida School District, "A hostile parent can make statements, threats, and also display feelings that are very difficult for an administrator to work through. Administrators are certainly affected by these unsuccessful attempts to rectify the situation, however they also want to continue to pursue a solution to the problem. Administrators need to be heard and reassured after these situations. They may also need to hear objective recommendations in regard to their safety, if it is being compromised. By replenishing their resolve, we actually continue what is best for the kids."

Here are several of my own practical recommendations that may prove helpful after an especially taxing parental encounter:

- ◆ Go to your room! Well, maybe your office sounds a little more professional. Don't attempt to engage in another activity immediately after a conflict. This is the time for a quick time-out. It's easy to want to immediately sort out what just occurred or decide what your next step will be. These issues can be addressed in a minute. For now, your emotional state is most important. Get something to drink and at least attempt to relax. It's an opportune time to regain your composure if it indeed was shaken.

- ◆ Try to jot down thoughts and immediate concerns that arose during the meeting. Don't trust memory, since attempting to recall portions of the meeting at a later date may in itself cause stress. Statements made by the parent as well as the administrator's response can be important in the future. Note any threats, use of vulgarity, or other pertinent statements made by the parent. This is one of the reasons that I strongly recommend that another colleague attend the meeting if at all possible.

♦ Talk to someone. Whether it's your principal, assistant principal, guidance counselor, or trusted colleague, attempt to talk to someone about the experience. Be aware of your feelings that could understandably include anger, confusion, disbelief, or fear.

♦ Contact your superior. Whether it is your superintendent, general director, area director, and so on. Whoever is "above" you, contact them! Fortunately, this is an option that school administrators instinctively seem to use and rightly so, since it serves two purposes. First, it enables school administrators to vent their feelings regarding the situation. Second, it gives administrators peace of mind knowing that their superiors know exactly what happened before the parent can make unfounded allegations against them.

After a conflict, I always emphasize the importance of talking to someone, whether informally or formally. No administrator has ever benefited from carrying around stress due to a turbulent parental encounter. This pertains to beginning administrators and administrators with extensive experience. I've discovered that more experienced administrators tend to talk to colleagues and their superiors immediately after their encounters with confrontational or aggressive parents.

Tom M. has been an assistant principal for approximately four years in a Florida senior high school. He explained, "When I first started as an administrator, a parent didn't agree with a decision that I made concerning his son. The parent claimed racism, and I took that attack personally. I used several colleagues for sounding boards and really vented. What a relief! Ironically I found out that this same father had similar "run ins" with the other administrators. Now, after an incident with a particularly troublesome parent, I usually meet with my colleagues as a debriefing period."

Roy S. has been a Florida school district administrator for 12 years. He noted, "When I first started as an administrator, I attempted to break up a fight and was punched in the temple. I ignored this incident and never sat down and talked about it. This bothered me. Now, if I am involved in any type of altercation, especially one involving a hostile parent, I find my colleagues and I get the incident off my chest. It really helps me."

Fortunately, school administrators can take simple steps to possibly reduce stress and one way is through debriefing. Unfortunately, it's often easy for school administrators to overlook this important task. The benefits of debriefing far outweigh however, the brief time spent in this valuable endeavor.

Discussion

1. Have instances of parental aggression affected you physically, emotionally, or cognitively? If so, how have you addressed this issue?

2. Do you have the opportunity to debrief after a turbulent encounter with a parent? If so, how is the debriefing conducted?

3. Do you feel that formal or informal debriefings are essential for school administrators after an altercation with a hostile parent? Why or why not are you of this opinion?

9

Three Levels From Which To Address Parental Aggression

Parental aggression can be addressed through the implementation of specialized techniques and the avoidance of common mistakes and simple oversights. In addition, there are three seldom-mentioned sources from which to address the issue of parental aggression. The first source is at the university level, the second source is at the school district level, and third source, the school level.

The University Level

Educational administration as a field has been criticized for the way in which individuals are prepared for positions in school leadership, possibly since universities are pressured to accept adequate quantities of candidates to justify their program's cost and existence (Sarason, 1999). The result is the admission of individuals of borderline quality with continued dependence on traditional selection criteria including Graduate Record Examination (GRE) grade point average and letters of recommendation. This issue is especially important since it is projected that approximately 50 percent of current school administrators will exit the nation's schools in the next decade (Harris, Arnold, Lowery, & Crocker, 2000).

Now more than ever it is crucial for institutions of higher learning to attract and select high quality candidates to school leadership preparation programs (Creighton & Jones, 2001). In addition, the question remains as to whether current admission standards are high enough to attract the most capable candidates to these preparatory programs (Norton, 1994). Taking into consideration these alarming facts, it would not be farfetched to surmise that difficulties dealing with aggressive parents may be related to lack of skills attained in these preparation programs and the overall quality of administrators that emanate from these programs. Fortunately, a "window of opportunity" exists to dramatically improve the quality of education (Creighton & Jones, p. 6), especially in light of the massive exit of school administrators from the field of education in the near future.

Creighton and Jones (2001) conducted an interesting study which determined the extent to which rigorous selection processes existed within administrator preparation programs and identified exemplary models which resulted in the selection of candidates who possessed strong qualifications and school leadership characteristics.

Among their discoveries:

Finding 1: Only 3 percent of programs required the student's bachelor degree to be in education or one strong in liberal arts. The GRE is the most prevalent criteria used for the selection of candidates into administrator preparatory programs. Cutoff scores adversely affect a large number of prospective graduate students.

Finding 2: Students that entered educational administration preparatory programs between 1996 and 1999 attained GRE scores that ranked third from the bottom when compared with 41 graduate fields. Also, compared with seven specific education majors, students who majored in education administration ranked second to last in verbal reasoning, third from last in quantitative reasoning, and second from last in analytical reasoning.

Finding 3: Only 6 percent of the university preparatory programs required personal interviews as part of the selection process. Unfortunately, the interview was considered the most important administrator screening tool (Baltzell & Dentler, 1983; Bryant, 1978; Pounder & Young, 1996; Schmitt & Cohen, 1990).

Finding 4: The majority of the universities studied permitted candidates to complete their master's degree in educational administration without satisfying the teaching requirement (two to three years in most states) for state certification of principal or superintendent.

Finding 5: Eighty percent of the universities provided conditional admissions policies, usually if students' GRE were below normal acceptance levels.

It is suggested that leadership be viewed as more of a performing art than a set of skills, knowledge, or competencies (Sarason, 1999; Vaill, 1989). One recommendation made by Sarason (1999) is the inclusion of auditions in the selection of potential school administrators. Auditions differ from interviews in that interviews focus on a set of predetermined or hypothetical questions that permit candidates to explain how they would effectively deal with situations. Auditions offer the candidate the opportunity to immerse into the real life environment of administration. The candidate is required to actually demonstrate a behavior. Although not considered a performance, the university personnel can observe if the candidate displays the qualities or potential necessary for dealing effectively with students, school personnel, or parents.

In addition, the candidate's level of sensitivity, inventiveness, and spontaneity, can be examined. I found this interesting since these aforementioned traits are all essential for interacting with aggressive parents.

Creighton and Jones (2001) explain that auditions are not without their disadvantages. For example, they are time consuming, labor intensive, and overly subjective to judgment and decisions by university personnel. The authors noted, however, "program leaders must strive for consistent evaluations and objective decisions based on quality of performance and display of leadership" (p. 22).

Ted Creighton, a professor of educational administration at Sam Houston State University states,

> Why is it assumed that high quality effective administrators can be produced by university programs without first attracting and selecting candidates with existing potential of school administration and leadership? And why do Institutions of Higher Learning still utilize the common nonbehavior-based selection criteria that show no evidence of relationship with leadership skills, knowledge, or disposition? (Creighton & Jones, 2001, p. 28–29)

Creighton concludes, "until all parties involved seriously address the selection of candidates with strong analytical ability, high administrative potential, and demonstrated success in teaching, the education profession will continue to be a refuge for mediocre candidates" (p. 29). *By no means do I imply that school administrators experience difficulties with parents because they are incompetent.* I am of the opinion, however, that engaging volatile parents necessitates the use of specialized skills and these skills can be taught at the university level.

School District Level

Currently, a popular buzz phrase for school administrators is "school violence prevention." The effects of Columbine and several other school tragedies piqued the attention of school districts nationwide, and rightly so, as campus safety was redefined as priority one. School districts have made great efforts to provide training and increase the overall awareness of school administrators to the contagion of student perpetrated school violence. Unfortunately, frequently overlooked in these efforts has been the examination of other types of school related violence, including violence perpetrated by parents.

During my second study on parental aggression, I asked school administrators to respond to the following statement, "I feel more threatened by hostile parents than I did two or three years ago." I discovered that 52 percent of administrators agreed with this statement. This dramatically indicated that school districts should consider a separate examination of this issue and subsequently accord the issue the attention that it demands.

To further emphasize my opinion, I also asked administrators to respond to the following statement, "Parental hostility/aggression is an issue that requires more attention from my school district." Again, 68 percent "strongly agreed" with this statement. It is very probable that school districts could be overlooking the opportunity to assist their administrators regarding this critical issue.

Our nation's school districts also establish civility policies in an effort to manage behaviors within and around scholastic settings. Alarmingly, school civility policies have been scarce, as we will discuss in Chapter 11.

With a heightened awareness and sensitivity toward school violence prevention, the issue of parental aggression may auspiciously garner attention from school districts that have previously been ignored, whether intentionally or unintentionally. It's also possible that school districts haven't actually ignored the issue of parental aggression, but simply been unaware of the acuteness of the issue. Subsequently, the responsibility to inform and educate school boards and superintendents regarding parental aggression actually may be assumed by school administrators.

Candy Olsen is a school board member in the Hillsborough County school district, which is currently the 12th largest school district in America. She explains,

> We strive to improve each school's climate because we know it improves learning when we provide a safe and orderly environment. While most of our attention has been focused on children and some attention has been paid to teachers, few of us have been aware of the stunning number of incidents involving parental aggression toward administra-

tors. If we seek to provide a safe and orderly environment for all, we adults must all model and expect respect toward one another. As we train our administrators in the many facets of their jobs, we need to consider including strategies for dealing with parental bullies.

The School Level

During the course of this book, I hope that I have challenged the perception that parental aggression is an obscure topic, and unworthy of attention. I discovered that the issue of parental aggression is indeed viewed as a legitimate problem by administrators themselves. Subsequently, like any other critical issue confronting our nation's schools, plans should be considered for the eradication, or at least analysis, of the problem of parental aggression.

Efforts at the university and school district level could still limit the opportunity for school-based administrators to affect immediate change. The question then remains, "Where can school administrators directly address the issue of parental aggression?" Truthfully, I think it is within their own schools!

Many administrators invest time becoming proficient in techniques to effectively handle confrontational or aggressive parents but they err when they attempt to address the problem single-handedly. The problem is best addressed as a school based effort, a problem similar to drug abuse, student violence, or sexual abuse.

I recommend that school administrators provide in-service programs for school personnel regarding parental aggression at the beginning of each school year. This is practical since parents interact with administrators on a year-round basis, and the sooner knowledge is gained, the better for all involved. In-services should include selected staff, including fellow administrators, office personnel, and school resource officers.

School administrators remain at the forefront of incidences relating to parental aggression. By preparing for their own involvement with aggressive parents prior to the confrontation, many complications could be avoided. Likewise, administrators who involve their staffs in this issue can substantially reduce the occurrence or severity of these volatile encounters.

Discussion

1. In your opinion, do universities adequately train future school leaders for interactions with volatile individuals, including aggressive parents?

2. Is your school district cognizant of the issue of parental aggression toward school administrators? If they are, what has been done to address this problem?

3. What could you do (or have you done) to address the problem of parental aggression within your own school?

10

The Results
of My Studies

Several individuals have addressed the topic of parental aggression toward school administrators. Storey (1990) identified a range of conflicts that occurred between parents and their children's schools. Margolis (1990) studied the origins of parent-school conflict and identified, (a) common errors that exacerbate these difficulties, (b) strategies for resolving conflicts and improving relationships, and (c) alternate courses of action if these approaches are not successful. Margolis & Tewell (1988) argued that if administrators personalize attacks, defend themselves, or argue with detractors, an escalation of anger and deterioration of the situation could result. He also offered several options for dealing with parental conflict.

As I began my own exploration into the area of parental aggression and school administrators, I discovered that there were not extensive journal articles, papers, or magazine articles available on this topic. Much of the research related to parental aggression toward school administrators has been anecdotal in nature. I found little to no actual empirical research on this topic, and for me that situation posed advantages and disadvantages. I considered the advantages of a possible research effort—excitement and opportunity to explore an issue that for the most part was not researched. The main disadvantage was the complicated choice of which specific areas to actually pursue in my research. I must admit my main trepidation was the possibility that I would find that administrators had little or no interest in this topic.

While considering a direction for my research, I discovered myself desiring the answers to three specific questions. First, what were the various types of parental aggression that school administrators were encountering? Second, how frequently were administrators encountering these specific types of parental aggressions? And third, what factors (administrative and school level) were associated with acts of parental aggression? Quite simply, I wanted to know what exactly was occurring, how frequently it was occurring, and what was making it occur. My initial research study was conducted at the school district level, and the second study was conducted at the state level.

A District Level Study of Parental Aggression

My initial study was conducted in the 12th largest school district in the United States. The district enrolled approximately 160,000 students and employed 653 school administrators. All 191 schools in the district were included in the study. Elementary, middle, secondary, and other school settings, that is, alternative and exceptional education, were also included.

I developed a self-report measure, The School Administrator Parent Aggression Survey (SAPAS). The survey allowed me to compile information regarding the frequency and type of aggression perpetrated against school administrators by parents during the 1997–98 school year. My trepidation that school administrators would find little interest in the topic quickly diminished as I received a 50 percent response rate.

I formed three categories of parental aggression to be included on the SAPAS:

1. Verbal threats and intimidation (V)

2. Noncontact threats and intimidation (N)

3. Physical contact (P)

The following statements are contained on the SAPAS. (The letters following the statements indicate whether the statement indicates a verbal threat, noncontact threat, or physical contact). School administrators were asked to indicate the *number of times* each type of aggression was directed toward them.

- Parents threatened to contact "other authorities," that is, school board. (V)
- Shouting or profanity was directed at me by a parent/guardian. (V)
- A parent leveled false accusations against me. (V)
- Verbal threats/intimidation were made against my physical well-being by a parent. (V)
- I was present when another school employee was physically confronted by a parent. (P)
- A parent intentionally invaded my "personal space." (N)
- A parent physically blocked my path of entry or exit. (N)
- A parent threw an object (i.e., pencil, paper) in an attempt to injure/ intimidate me. (P)
- A parent made actual physical contact with me, that is, hit, kicked, or shoved. (P)

Several interesting findings emerged from the survey:

- *On two or more occasions, 71 percent* of administrators received a threat by parents/guardians to contact "other authorities" (i.e., school board, attorneys).
- Approximately *50 percent* of school administrators reported that shouting or profanity was directed toward them by a parent during the school year.

♦ *Fifty-eight percent* of administrators reported that parents or guardians leveled at least one false accusation against them during the school year.

♦ Fifteen percent of the administrators reported at least once during the school year, a parent intentionally blocked their personal space.

A State Level Study of Parental Aggression

My second study was conducted by surveying a large sample of administrators throughout the state of Florida. Once again, I was relieved to receive a response rate of over 50 percent. The state of Florida can be easily generalized to most states, since its school districts are adequate representations of urban, rural, and suburban schools throughout the nation. The socioeconomic levels of Florida's school districts also are well represented. Surveys were sent to 669 principals and assistant principals in Florida's 67 school districts.

Once again, the SAPAS was administered for the statewide study, however an additional 13-item Likert scale, the SAAS (The School Administrator Attitude Scale) allowed me to explore school administrator attitudes regarding various statements pertaining to parental aggression (see Appendix).

This statewide study also produced several interesting findings. Most notable was the discovery that school administrators were indeed experiencing an excessive amount of verbal aggression from parents. Findings included:

♦ Shouting or profanity was directed at 60 percent of administrators on at least two occasions during the school year.

♦ During the school year, 41 percent of the administrators received verbal threats or intimidation against their physical well-being by parents.

♦ Seventy percent of the school administrators had false accusations leveled against them by parents on at least one occasion during the school year, while 30 percent of the administrators were falsely accused on three or more occasions.

♦ During the school year, 79 percent of administrators, on three or more occasions, reported receiving parental threats to contact "other authorities," that is, school boards, attorneys, and so on.

♦ During the school year 26 percent of administrators reported that a parent intentionally invaded their personal space.

♦ Thirty-five percent of administrators observed another school employee being physically confronted by a parent.

I then examined administrator attitudes regarding the issue of parental aggression using the SAAS. (This scale was not included in the district level study). I discovered that:

♦ *Seventy-one percent* of the administrators agreed or strongly agreed that parental aggression was an issue that required more attention from their school districts.

♦ *Seventy-six percent* of the administrators agreed or strongly agreed that their administrative colleagues have voiced their concerns regarding parental aggression.

♦ *Five and four-tenths percent* of the school administrators agreed or strongly agreed that they felt more threatened now by hostile parents than they did 2 to 3 years ago.

♦ *Thirty-five percent* of school administrators agreed or strongly agreed that they felt vulnerable to parental aggression.

I also took the opportunity to ask the school leaders to provide input regarding their approaches toward aggressive hostile parents. I found that:

♦ *Forty-two percent* of administrators either agreed or strongly agreed that they altered their approaches with parents due to previous encounters with hostile parents.

- *Fifty-eight percent* of administrators either disagreed or strongly disagreed that they *would not* conduct a meeting with a parent who was considered hostile.

- *Sixty-nine percent* of administrators agreed or strongly agreed that it was necessary to have other school personnel in a room when meeting with a hostile parent.

- *Eighty-six percent* of administrators agreed or strongly agreed that they felt free discussing their experiences (with hostile parent) with their superiors.

I concluded from these studies that parental aggression is certainly being experienced by many school leaders. Verbal aggression was the most evident form of aggression. I found it alarming that over 50 percent of the administrators had been the target of shouting or profanity during the school year on more than two occasions. Also disturbing, was the fact that over 70 percent of the school leaders received threats by parents to contact "other authorities."

In light of these discoveries, I feel confident concluding that:

- School leaders consider the issue of parental aggression a genuine concern.

- School leaders report that instances of verbal aggression occur frequently.

- School leaders feel that the issue of parental aggression should be addressed by their school districts.

I have only provided a portion of the statistics produced by my two studies. I have included only the results that would possibly pique the interest of school administrators. Figure 10.1 provides additional information regarding the state level study.

Discussion

1. In this chapter, were there any statistics that surprised you? How did these results differ from your presumptions?

2. The results of my two studies exposed a significant degree of parental verbal aggression in the form of threats, accusations, and shouting/profanity. Have you experienced this type of aggression from parents within your own school?

3. In your opinion, is parental aggression a genuine problem? Do you think that it occurs too frequently? Should your school district address this problem to a greater extent?

11

Support and Civility for the Bad Guys

Do you remember the principal that I mentioned in the Introduction? He was the administrator who was verbally accosted by the imposing parent in the parking lot after school. During the year it took me write this book, he decided to change job positions. I was almost certain that the episode with the "parking lot parent" was the last straw for him. I'm happy to report, however, that he changed jobs for reasons other than being aggravated by that particular parent. I found it interesting that during the period that I conducted my research, this principal spoke more frequently of his interactions with aggressive and confrontational parents during the course of his long, impressive career. As a matter of fact, during that year many school leaders spoke to me about their experiences with aggressive and confrontational parents. I was always glad to hear, "It is about time someone looked into this issue." It was a great opportunity for me to "pick the brains" of school leaders regarding a topic that I originally thought might have generated little interest.

During the year, I formed many relationships with school administrators and educators throughout the country, as I solicited advice, asked for quotes, and spoke at conferences. As I engaged in these activities, my colleagues from around the nation thoughtfully informed me of their participation in actual situations when parental aggression was evident. I gratefully collected the media clippings sent from administrators and continued to search for any news that pertained to aggression toward school leaders. I was amazed at the number and types of occurrences. I discovered that one superintendent was actually murdered at work, and another administrator was kidnapped by parents before he was eventually rescued. One magazine editor directed me to a news story that described a situation where a high school student was stabbed, and his parents subsequently returned to the school seeking revenge. The parents refused to leave the campus as requested and proceeded to become engaged in a physical altercation with school personnel. I wondered if the RAID approach would have been useful during that situation.

In every reported instance of parental aggression, it occurred to me that these parents reacted in that manner because they simply were not getting what they wanted at the time or felt that they or their child had been wronged. Admittedly, not every school administrator was brutalized by parents in as dramatic a manner as reported in the media, but in my opinion, most episodes of parental aggression result in school leaders being affected in a negative manner. Parental aggression differs from student-initiated aggression for reasons that I have described earlier in this book. Administrators are sometimes viewed as the "bad guys" on campus, since they enforce school policy, and these policies are not always popular with the school population or parents. I think that most school administrators accept this fact and are not hindered by this negative perception since it is part of their job to enforce school policy. I did, however, detect frustration among school leaders with the "bad guy" image when it involved parents' perceptions of them. Administrators argue that parents should know better or be more knowledgeable of their role in the school. The fact that school leaders are occasionally labeled anything derogatory by a parent is frustrating, since the administrator's main goal is the success of each student. That doesn't seem to be something in which a "bad guy" would take interest. Coupled with the manner in which they are treated, it is easily understood why frustration exists among our nation's school administrators. Some administrators seem to maintain the stance that "parents might not get what they want, but that doesn't give them the right to target me for aggression." I could not agree with this statement more.

Have parents become more aggressive in the past several years? While I admit that misbehavior is something that will always be a topic of discussion in our schools, it seems to me and many educators that parents are reacting more forcefully than ever before. We say the same regarding student violence. During the 1980s and 1990s, there were hardly incidences of the intensity as the Columbine and Jonesboro tragedies. The severity of the behaviors engaged in by students and parents—as currently observed by school leaders—were rarely seen or reported just a few short years ago. If indeed incidences of aggression occurred to this extent in past decades, maybe educators are now simply more sensitive, observant, or willing to report violent behavior in and around our nation's campuses. Maybe educators are now more aware of the potential for violence. I think that the events of September 11th have yet to be measured regarding the effect it will have on our nation's students and families. To be sure, who would blame school populations and parents if "on-edge" feelings were detected on our campuses? Does this on-edge feeling permeate relationships between school leaders and parents? Good questions, but that is another study for another day.

In the Introduction, I voiced my fear that the principal, as a result of parental conflict, would leave the field of education and as a result take away the talents he had to offer the school. The kids would ultimately be the losers. He did change positions, but not because of parental conflict, but how about other school leaders? I have communicated with some who continue to consider exiting the field due to parental conflicts. How do we keep them? Two ways may be to provide support for these administrators from their superiors, and the establishment of civility policies, which limit what an aggressive parent, can and cannot do. School administrators aren't the bad guys, they are usually good people carrying out unpopu-

bad guys, they are usually good people carrying out unpopular decisions based on the good of the overall school population.

Is Anybody Up There?

I have become cognizant of a strong opinion that many school administrators maintain regarding parental aggression. The opinion is, "It makes all the difference in the world when we have support from 'up top.'" This can be interpreted as support from their superiors, that is, principals, general directors, superintendents, or school boards. Some school leaders express confidence in knowing that their superiors will support them during encounters with confrontational or aggressive parents.

Other administrators have informed me that they become totally demoralized when their superiors fail to "back them up," especially when they are certain that their actions, decisions, or remarks to parents are justified. As a result, administrators could easily adopt attitudes that are counterproductive to conflict resolution. One attitude could include, "give the parents what they want, because it's not worth the aggravation. Besides, it doesn't really matter what I say because they'll just go to the next level." Unfortunately, in many cases this is indeed true. Parents have the ability to shift a conflict that could be handled at the school to the next level, that is, school boards, to receive satisfaction if they are in the least bit perturbed with the actions or demeanor of a school administrator. As a result, school administrators may feel offended, but also become apathetic, knowing that their opinion means little when compared to an aggressive parent's path to resolution. Optimally, school leaders should feel that their efforts are for the benefit of the children, while at the same time keeping in mind the common good of the school population. While all parents should have a voice in their children's education, it is unfortunate that their aggressive demeanors may ultimately influence decisions. An assistant principal once explained to me that "when I meet with an aggressive parent, it makes all the difference in the world when I know I've made the right decision, have conveyed that decision to the parent, and know that I have support from my superiors."

Crossing the Line

A friend of mine—who also coaches high school football—discovered that I was in the process of conducting research on the issue of parental aggression. He amusingly related a personal story of how, during a football game, he turned his head and was shocked to discover an irate parent who began to berate him about the fact that his son was not playing in the game. My dumbstruck friend, caught totally off guard, just listened. After his tirade, the parent returned to the bleachers, where most parents sit during football games. My friend, not so amusingly, proceeded to ask me why there wasn't a policy that protected or limited a parent's actions in cases such as this. I couldn't answer him, but agreed with his concern that this parent could have easily had worse intentions than that of simply yelling at him.

Ironically, shortly after this conversation, I was asked to participate on a civility committee for my school district. During the 2001–2002 school year, I searched the many school districts in the state of Florida for an existing civility policy. I was amazed to discover that there was only one district that had an established policy. As I spoke at conferences around the nation during the school year, I was again very surprised to discover that very few audience members were employed in school districts that had established civility policies. No civility policies? As hard as it was to believe, it was true. Thankfully, our district soon established a policy that was constructed with input from educators, students, community members, and parents. We established a document that enabled us to "draw a line" regarding acceptable conduct within and around our district's campuses. At first, I wondered how a civility policy could actually affect a hostile parent's behavior, but I soon discovered its value.

One afternoon, I was walking down the hallway of a high school and noticed a parent standing in front of the assistant principal's offices. She could be best described as livid. In her proximity were students and her young son and daughter. I asked if I could assist her, and she belligerently informed me that she had requested that a student assistant summon her daughter from class. She was upset that this process was taking too long. The parent "made a scene" to the extent that I considered her disruptive. I proceeded to the student affairs office and notified the assistant principal, who, accompanied by the school resource officer, confronted the mother. The school resource officer firmly informed the mother that her behavior would lead to repercussions if she did not immediately exit the campus. The mother continued to argue unsuccessfully with the school resource officer and was close to being arrested. She questioned why she couldn't disagree with the fact that her behavior was disruptive. I then proceeded to point to the wall where our newly formed civility policy proudly hung. She read the statement and then seemed to stop in her tracks. She realized that she was "crossing the line" in regard to her behavior. The policy was something tangible to the mother, and that may have prevented further conflict. I would like to think that in this instance, our civility policy made the difference.

Of course, there will always be individuals, including parents, who couldn't care less about any civility policy. Nonetheless, these policies should be established. I also caution that the establishment of a civility policy will not guarantee that behaviors will change immediately. It takes time for any civility policy to take effect. Patience, however, will result in established mindsets that allow individuals to know where that line is regarding their behavior, whatever that behavior may be.

According to Critical Incident Associates, there are several factors that may contribute to school place violence, including:

- ♦ A weak or nonexistent policy against all forms of violence
- ♦ No clearly defined rules of conduct
- ♦ A nonexistent or weak mechanism for reporting violent or threatening behavior

The institute also notes a failure to take immediate action against those individuals who threaten or commit acts of violence. The parent who berated my friend during the football game was basically told to return to his seat. I wonder if this simple action was enough to dissuade the parent from acting in this manner during another game.

The establishment of civility policies and the patience to stick with them are of the utmost importance to school districts in their efforts to foster mutual respect within schools and between schools and parents. Coupled with support from their superiors, school leaders can address the actions of aggressive parents with less aggravation and much more confidence. It might also be easier to accept being unfairly viewed as the "bad guy."

Discussion

1. Have you been supported by your superiors when involved in a conflict with an aggressive parent who takes it to the "next level"?

2. Does your school district have an established civility policy? Are you satisfied with the status of the policy?

3. How would you make your school district's civility policy visible to your student population and the overall community, including parents?

12

A
"Disclaimer"
About Parents

Much of this book has examined the unenviable position that school administrators sometimes find themselves, that is, being involved in situations where they must skillfully and effectively interact with aggressive parents. Although I explored the value of parental participation in the school setting, this book has for the most part focused on aggressive parents and not aggressive school administrators.

While this book focused on a minority of individuals, the fact remains that this small population of people can also make life extra challenging for school leaders who must deal with a multitude of other difficulties on a daily basis. I find it interesting that when asked, school leaders can immediately recall their most volatile confrontations with parents. These memories endure—but why? That particular topic is beyond the scope of this book, but it's apparent that a few bad experiences, with a few difficult parents, often make a lasting impression on our school leaders.

I want to emphasize that the great majority of parents that I've dealt with in my 18-year career have truly been wonderful people with their children's best interests in mind. I imagine that most school administrators probably feel the same way. There are few things more satisfying professionally than a parent who is a real "fan" of yours, who trusts your judgment and educational expertise. These parents are truly gems that school administrators love to collect, and they can make a tough job a lot more enjoyable.

I mentioned the term "bad guys" in regard to the manner in which school administrators may be perceived by students or parents. Obviously, this tongue-and-cheek expression usually has little or no basis, but school leaders should likewise also use caution to avoid viewing the parent as the "bad guy." It would be wonderful if there was no evidence of "good guy versus bad guy," scenarios within our school walls. I hope that this book has shed some light on the possible reasons for these behaviors, since there exists a reason for every individual's behavior, including the most difficult parents. Fortunately, many savvy school leaders are aware of this fact and at least attempt to temper their reaction to these individuals, no matter how difficult that task may be.

Finally, like the parents that I have interacted with throughout my career, I share a similar respect toward the school administrators with whom I've had the pleasure of interacting. Although I thought that I realized the enormous responsibility that they bear during the course of a school year, this project has even increased my appreciation and admiration for these leaders.

Who has greater responsibilities in our society than educators and parents? In my opinion, the two virtues necessary to be successful at either endeavor are patience and understanding. School leaders must possess large quantities of both virtues since their positions will inherently provide ample opportunity to come in contact with the most difficult of individuals.

Discussion

1. How much effort did it take to resolve parental conflicts during the most recent school year? Do you think the effort was worth it?

2. Has a parent ever perceived you as a "bad guy" during your administrative career? How well have you dealt with this perception?

3. Why do parents who are "fans" of yours hold you in such high esteem? As a school administrator, when you are engaged in a parental conflict, what are your most noteworthy attributes?

Appendix

Figure 10.1. Descriptive Statistics for School Administrator Parent Aggression Survey

		Total	*Elementary*	*Middle*	*Secondary*
		(n = 338)	*(n = 126)*	*(n = 93)*	*(n = 98)*
(12) Shouting/ profanity was directed at me by a parent/ guardian.	M	2.06	2.03	2.36	1.77
	SD	1.53	1.50	1.50	1.58
	0	23.2%	22.4%	17.4%	30.6%
	1	17.3	18.4	13.0	20.4
	2	17.9	16.8	20.7	16.3
	3	14.0	18.4	14.1	7.1
	4+	27.7	24.0	34.8	25.5

(13) Verbal threats/ intimidation were made against my phys- ical well- being by a par- ent/guardian.	M	0.74	0.75	0.85	0.61
	SD	1.10	1.15	1.15	0.98
	0	60.2%	62.7%	54.3%	64.6%
	1	17.7	14.3	21.7	16.7
	2	13.5	13.5	13.0	13.5
	3	5.1	4.8	6.5	3.1
	4+	3.6	4.8	4.3	2.1
(14) False accusations were leveled against me by a parent/ guardian.	M	1.73	1.44	1.91	1.92
	SD	1.48	1.42	1.48	1.53
	0	28.9%	34.9%	23.9%	24.7%
	1	20.2	23.8	18.5	19.6
	2	20.2	18.3	22.8	20.6
	3	10.4	7.9	12.0	9.3
	4+	20.2	15.1	22.8	25.8
(15) A parent/ guardian threatened to contact "other authorities", i.e., school board, attorneys, etc.	M	3.36	3.18	3.54	3.44
	SD	1.07	1.22	0.78	1.05
	0	3.0%	4.8%	0.0%	3.1%
	1	5.4	8.0	1.1	5.1
	2	11.9	13.6	14.1	8.2
	3	12.5	11.2	14.1	12.2
	4+	67.3	62.4	70.7	71.4

(16) A parent/ guardian made actual contact with me (hit, kicked, shoved, etc.).	M	0.01	0.008	0.01	0.01
	SD	0.11	0.089	0.10	0.10
	0	98.8%	99.2%	98.9%	99.0%
	1	1.2	0.8	1.1	1.0
	2	0	0	0	0
	3	0	0	0	0
	4+	0	0	0	0
(17) A parent/ guardian threw an object (i.e., paper, pencil, etc.) in an attempt to injure or intimidate me.	M	0.02	0.04	0.00	0.02
	SD	0.20	0.29	0.00	0.14
	0	98.2%	97.6%	100.00%	98.0%
	1	1.5	1.6	0	2.0
	2	0	0	0	0
	3	0.3	0.8	0	0
	4+	0	0	0	0
(18) A parent/ guardian physically blocked my path of entry or exit.	M	0.13	0.14	0.09	0.16
	SD	0.46	0.50	0.28	0.55
	0	89.9%	89.7%	91.4%	89.8%
	1	8.0	7.9	8.6	6.1
	2	1.2	1.6	0	2.0
	3	0.6	0	0	2.0
	4+	0.3	0.8	0	0

(19) A parent/ guardian intentionally invaded my "personal space."	M	0.46	0.51	0.51	0.37
	SD	0.89	0.88	1.01	0.80
	0	73.3%	69.0%	73.9%	77.6%
	1	13.9	16.7	10.9	13.3
	2	8.0	9.5	8.7	5.1
	3	3.3	4.0	3.3	3.1
	4+	1.5	0.8	3.3	1.0
(20) I was present when another school employee was physically confronted by a parent.	M	0.73	0.58	0.84	0.84
	SD	1.18	1.05	1.31	1.23
	0	64.1%	68.3%	64.1%	59.2%
	1	15.1	17.5	9.8	17.3
	2	10.1	6.3	13.0	10.2
	3	5.0	4.0	4.3	7.1
	4+	5.6	4.0	8.7	6.1

References

Baltzell, D.,& Denler, R. (1983). *Selecting american school principals: Research report.* Cambridge, MA: Alt Publishing.

Benjamin, L. (1987). Understanding and managing stress in the academic world. *Highlights: An ERIC/CAPS Digest.* (ERIC Document Reproduction Service No. ED291017)

Black, S. (1998). Parent support. *The American School Board Journal, 185*(4), 50–53.

Blauvelt, P. (2001). *Inside School Safety: Effective Management Strategies for School Administrators, 6*(2),1–12.

Bradley, A. (1999). Parents express scant interest in helping govern schools. *Education Week, 18*(28), 5.

Bryant, B. J. (1978). *Employment factors superintendents use in hiring administrators for their school districts.* Prepared for the Association for School, College, & University Staffing. (ERIC Document Reproduction Service No.ED 9866)

Bulach, C. R. (1993). A measure of openness and trust. *People In Education, 1*(4). (ERIC Document Reproduction Service No.ED506 570)

Bulach, C., Pickett, W., & Boothe, D. (1998). *Mistakes educational leaders make.* (ERIC Document Reproduction Service No. ED 422604).

Chapko, M. A., & Buchko, M. (2001). Surviving the principalship. *Principal, 80*(4), 38–39.

Checkley, K. (2000). Parents are people too: Leading with empathy and compassion. *Educational Update, 42*(7).

Creighton, T., & Jones, G. (2001, August). *Selection or self-selection? How rigorous are selection criteria in education administration programs?* Paper presented at the National Council of Professors of Educational Administration Conference.

Critical Incident Associates. Telephone interview with Larry Chavez, July 5, 2002.

Davis, S. H. (1997). The principal's paradox: Remaining secure in a precarious position. *NASSP Bulletin, 81*(592), 73–80.

Deutch, M. (1992). Building a community for learning: Typical responses to conflict. *Educational Leadership, 50*(1), p.16.

Egan, G. (1975). *The skilled helper: A model for systematic helping and interpersonal relating.* Monterey,CA: Brooks/Cole.

Egan,G. (1976). *Interpersonal living: A skills/contract approach to human-relations training in groups.* Monterey,CA: Brooks/Cole.

Elgin, S. H. (2000). *The gentle art of verbal self defense at work.* Paramus, NJ: Prentice-Hall.

Fege, A. F. (2000). From fund raising to hell raising: New roles for parents. *Educational Leadership, 57*(7), 39–43.

Harris, S., Arnold, M., Lowery, S., & Crocker, C. (2000). A study of motivators and inhibitors for men and women deciding to become a principal. *Education Leadership Review, 1*(3), 30–37.

Hester, H. (1989). Start at home to improve home-school relations. *NASSP Bulletin, 73*(513), 23–27.

Margolis, H. (1990). What to do when you're verbally attacked: The critical moment. *NASSP Bulletin, 74*(523), 34–38.

Margolis, H., & Tewell, K. J. (1988). Resolving conflict with parents: A guide for administrators. *NASSP Bulletin, 72*(506), 1–8.

Mc Ewan, E. K. (1998). *How to deal with parents who are angry, troubled, afraid, or just plain crazy.* Thousand Oaks, CA: Corwin Press.

Mitchell, J. T., & Everly, G. S. (1995). *Critical incident stress debriefing: An operations manual for the prevention of trauma among emergency service and disaster workers* (2nd ed.). Baltimore, MD: Chevron.

Norton, M. S. (1994). *Student recruitment and selection practices in educational administration programs.* Arizona State University. (ERIC Document Reproduction Service No.ED 366 087)

Patrikakou, E., & Weissberg, R. P. (1999). The seven P's of school-family partnerships. *Education Week*, XVIII, 21, 36.

Pounder, D. G., & Young, I. P. (1996). Recruitment and selection of educational administrators: Priorities for today's schools. In K. Leithwood, J. Chapment, D. Corson, P. Hallinger, & A. Hart (Eds.), *International Handbook of Educational Leadership* (pp. 279–308). Boston: Kluwer.

Robbins, S. P. (1974). *Managing organizational conflict: A nontraditional approach*. Englewood Cliffs, NJ: Prentice-Hall.

Rucci, R. B. (1991). *Dealing with difficult people: A guide for educators*. (ERIC Document Reproduction Service No. ED 336 810)

Sarason, S. B. (1999). *Teaching as a performing art*. New York: Teachers College Press.

Schmitt, N., & Cohen, S. A. (1990). *Criterion-related validity of the National Association of Secondary School Principals Assessment Center*. Reston, VA: NASSP.

Solomon, M. (1990). *Working with difficult people*. Paramus, NJ: Prentice-Hall.

Storey, V. J. (1990). *Parent-school conflict: An exploratory study. Report of a research study*. (ERIC Document Reproduction Service No.ED 342109)

Vaill, P. V. (1989). *Managing as a performing art*. San Francisco: Jossey-Bass.

Young, B. A., & Smith, T. M.(1997). *Findings from the condition of education 1997: The social context of education*. Washington, DC: National Center of Education Statistics.